ACCOLADE TO AN ARTIS

The Life and Work of William Woodhouse 1857 – 1939

by

Pam Corder-Birch

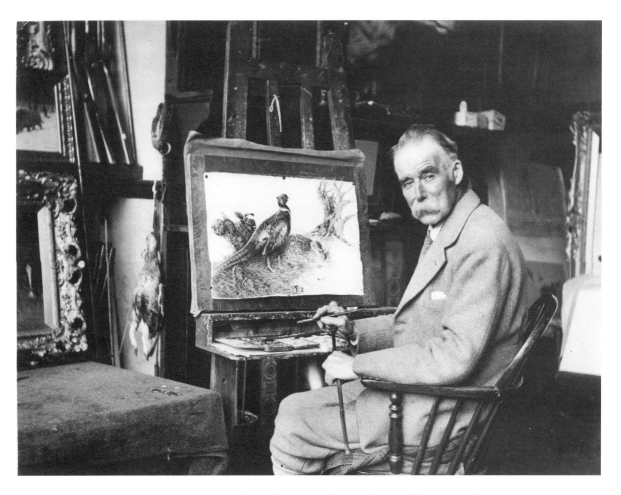

William Woodhouse in his studio at Auburn Court, Heysham circa 1930
Courtesy of Lancaster City Museums

Printed by

The Lavenham Press Ltd
Arbons House
47 Water Street
Lavenham
Suffolk
CO10 9RN

ISBN-10   0-9553537-0-X
ISBN-13   978-0-9553537-0-3

Further copies of this book are available from the Author / Publisher as above:

Price £12.95   plus P&P

Cheques and postal orders in English pounds sterling, payable to Mrs Corder-Birch.

CONTENTS

WILLIAM WOODHOUSE

by Pam Corder-Birch

INTRODUCTION

At an early age I fell in love with a painting. It was a pond surrounded by May blossom in full bloom, a heron was standing in the water awaiting his next meal and a moorhen was swimming unperturbed nearby. It was a scene that immediately conjured up an idyllic tranquillity, and I felt the artist must have a great affinity with his work.
The painting was signed W Woodhouse.

May Blossom. Watercolour.
From a private collection

Woodhouse was an unpretentious, modest craftsman who devoted his whole life to his work and created his own pictorial language. He was a good artist and his love for painting can be judged by its quality and quantity. Although he exhibited three times at the Royal Academy of Arts, London, little is known about him.

Woodhouse loved nature and the outdoor life. He liked to paint animals, birds, land and seascapes and was at his happiest when working around his native Morecambe Bay. His pictures were well composed: he captured the mood and spirit of his subjects whilst placing them in atmospheric surroundings to make them pleasing to the eye. Woodhouse was a perfectionist who would spend hours sketching in both pencil and watercolour before embarking on a final picture. It is this attention to detail that has made his work realistic and life-like.

Although tastes and fashions have changed since Woodhouse began his art career in the 1870's, his work continues to be appreciated and collected. His paintings can be found at auctions, private and public galleries, as well as at exhibitions. What greater **'Accolade to an Artist**' can there be, than to still have your work highly prized, collected and sought after?

Through Hogarth and Woodhouse family connections I have the pleasure of being distantly related to William Woodhouse. Therefore although this book is primarily about 'William Woodhouse the artist' there is a little about his family history too. (For those who like to dot the 'I's' and cross the 'T's', my great aunt was William Woodhouse's sister-in-law).

The last chapter is devoted to Roy Woodhouse: William's son, also an artist. Roy only took up art seriously after the First World War. He specialized in etchings and quickly gained a reputation, as his work was considered to be of the highest calibre.
Although Roy did not make a living from his art, I feel both he and his work are most definitely worthy of a mention.

One final point – to put the record straight!
Woodhouse has appeared in some books and on some web sites as William Arnold Woodhouse, which is incorrect. All official and family records refer to him as William Woodhouse and do not make any reference whatsoever to Arnold.

William Woodhouse - Acknowledgements.

When it comes to thanking all those who have helped me, the list is long and it is hard to single out any person, as everyone's contribution has assisted me to write and produce this book.

Sue Ashworth, now Projects Manager at Lancashire County Museum Service, (formerly Collections Manager: Lancaster City Museums) has been a wonderful support and inspiration to me with her expertise and knowledge about William Woodhouse and his work, and has very kindly allowed me access and use of material held at the museums. Despite a very heavy work schedule Sue has always made time to assist me on my visits to the museums. I should also like to thank Sue for writing the Foreword for this book.

Sue's colleague Paul Thompson, Museums Manager North, visited Winnie and Roy (Woodhouse's daughter and son) frequently and knew them well. I would like to thank Paul for his continued interest and encouragement in this publication.

Lynn Wilman, formerly at the Morecambe Reference Library, had a never-ending supply of local knowledge, she most diligently and enthusiastically answered all my queries. Nothing was too much trouble for Lynn and her former assistants.

Thanks too to the Librarians at the Harris Library, Preston. To Susan Wilson at the Lancaster Reference Library, for supplying information and copies of William Woodhouse material, which has been a tremendous help to me. To the Harris Museum and Art Gallery for their assistance, especially to Francis Marshall, the Keeper of their Fine Art Collection. To Glen Cooper, Editor of 'The Visitor' for keeping William Woodhouse 'alive' with reminiscences and anecdotes in his 'Looking Back' column.

I should like to thank Peter Wade: local historian, lecturer and author, for his useful tips and information about William Woodhouse. Also Mary Rawes and Thelma Simpson, who have both spent many hours researching the Woodhouse families of Poulton and Morecambe, and have passed on items of interest to me. Leslie and Margaret Morgan have welcomed me to their home; Leslie's personal interest in William Woodhouse and his friendship with Woodhouse's son Roy and daughter Winnie has been most useful.

I was fortunate enough to meet Bill Atkinson, who has long appreciated the work of local Lancashire artists. Bill's eye for a good picture combined with his in-depth knowledge of Woodhouse's work is quite awesome. I would therefore like to thank Bill for passing on some valuable pieces of information, which I have included in this book. Both Bill and his wife Kathleen have been most supportive throughout.

I would also like to thank Brian Garlick for kindly allowing me access to information he has collected about William Woodhouse and his work. It is evident that both Brian and his wife Kathleen have long admired both Woodhouse and his paintings.

I thank too my cousins Peter Hogarth, Martin Somers and Vega Sturgess. Peter for allowing me to use photographs he has taken of paintings, and Martin, a native of Morecambe for sharing his knowledge and love of the bay, it's traditions and customs, also his wife Angela, for always being kind and hospitable on my numerous visits. I thank Vega for her continuing interest in the history of the Hogarth and Woodhouse families and for the help she has given me.

A special thanks to Brian & Jill Fleming for assisting me with typing and layout.

To my good friend Penny Marks for her confidence in believing that I could complete this book and for her encouragement, my grateful thanks.

Finally I must thank the large band of Woodhouse admirers, who have allowed me to see and photograph their Woodhouse paintings, as well as those who have kindly sent me copies of their paintings for reproduction in this book. They are private collectors who wish to remain anonymous, but deserve a heartfelt thank you, as does my husband Adrian who has encouraged and helped me every step of the way. Last but not least I must thank Adrian, Sue Ashworth and my brother-in-law Phil Walker for proof reading my every word!

To all these and anyone I have inadvertently omitted to mention I give my grateful thanks.

Pam Corder-Birch.

A Special Acknowledgement.

From the moment the late Roy Gudgeon bought his first William Woodhouse painting he was hooked!

As an ardent admirer of Woodhouse's work, Roy soon met Winnie and a friendship was formed. Roy was eager to write a book about William Woodhouse and with Winnie's blessing he set about gathering all the information he could. Sadly the book was never finished before Roy's untimely death.

With my book well under way, a mutual friend put me in contact with Sheila Gudgeon, Roy's widow: she allowed me access to Roy's notes and papers and some 'gems' were unearthed which have enhanced this book. I would therefore like to thank Sheila for generously allowing me to use this material.

Pam Corder-Birch.

Foreword.

My colleague at the City Museum, Paul Thompson, introduced me to Miss Woodhouse, the artist's daughter, soon after I joined the museum in 1987. He had known Marie Winifred (Winnie) and her brother Roy for many years having met whilst staging a Woodhouse exhibition at the Museum in the early 1970s. Along with a number of loyal and devoted friends, Miss Woodhouse had kept the knowledge of and enthusiasm for this talented painter alive. It was an honour to meet this fascinating lady and learn about her father.

Woodhouse's skill in capturing the sheen on a dog's coat or the dappled sunlight on a bird's feathers was masterly. Today, however, his talent for showing the fruits of the hunt – or its likely quarry – are not universally appreciated, although they do still find considerable favour.

But work on our 1989 exhibition, marking the 50th Anniversary of the artist's death, showed Woodhouse was by no means limited to this subject matter. He was a lover of the British countryside and its wildlife with a fascination for the wider world. His taste for the exotic saw him paint leopards, tigers and camels. But he didn't ignore the harsh environments of the northern hemisphere as witnessed in his frozen scenes of wolves, bison and polar bears.

Woodhouse was technically accomplished too. His landscape watercolours were full of light and texture. His working sketches showed a true talent for swift observation and accuracy of line. His portraiture was sympathetic, sensitive and caring. How could he have been generally overlooked for so long?

Certainly his work was not avant-garde when one thinks of post First World War cutting-edge British artists like Graham Sutherland or John Nash. But not everyone was. Many artists continued to work in the figurative tradition with enviable success.

So, could it be that this figurative painter was missed because he chose to stay put on the Lancashire coast away from possible patrons? Would he have faired better in polite society in London? Who knows?

Whilst working on our exhibition, way back in 1989, it was clear more work was needed on Woodhouse to bring him back to public view. We had received great help with access to many paintings in private hands. Miss Woodhouse, too, gave us unlimited access to her photographs and private papers and to her father's many working sketches as well as generous helpings of her time, her information and her memories of her father, her family and her hometown of Morecambe at the time.

We had our hands full with our show, which proved a great success, but we felt this artist merited an authoritative publication too. We knew of one private researcher, Roy Gudgeon, working away on this in his spare time. He had raised the artist's name in occasional articles and we were keen to see his work come to fruition. Frankly, we were intrigued to see if he had unearthed caches of information and documentary evidence. We hoped he would succeed.

My own research was rich in personal stories and reminiscence but poor in hard evidence. It seemed, for example, that the student records for Lancaster School of Art no longer existed – or at least I failed to track them down. We very much looked forward to seeing the situation clarified and this deserving artist brought to wider public view.

Sadly Mr Gudgeon did not succeed in completing his work before his untimely death. Then Miss Woodhouse also died four days after her 101st birthday. Whilst her generosity persisted - with the bequest of her father's papers, sketches and a good number of his paintings - we feared there would be no easy way to bridge the gap and produce an authoritative volume on this under-rated artist.

Around three years ago the situation changed when Pam Corder-Birch came to the Museum to view Lancaster's holdings of works by Woodhouse. This new connection was instantly encouraging. The fruits of Pam's labours are here for you to see. With a wealth of family history knowledge and evidence at hand and many, many months of hard fact finding, checking and double - checking Pam has brought together a valuable, informative and much needed book on William Woodhouse.

Hopefully this book will now bring a talented artist to wider public view, at last. Although Woodhouse is held in high regard in this region he deserves far greater recognition. We feel he is one of Morecambe's best-kept secrets and so it is with great pleasure that we welcome its arrival.

Sue Ashworth
Project Manager: Lancashire County Museum Service.
(Formerly Collections Manager: Lancaster City Museums).

William Woodhouse as a young man.
Courtesy of Lancaster City Museums

CHAPTER 1

WILLIAM WOODHOUSE – A glimpse at his life.

1857 – 1939

This account of the life of William Woodhouse begins with his birth on the 1st October 1857 at Morecambe Street, Poulton, Lancashire. The third child and first son of James Woodhouse and Hannah nee Baxter, William was baptized at Holy Trinity Church, Poulton on 29th November 1857. (Poulton or Poulton-le-Sands, today forms part of the seaside resort of Morecambe).

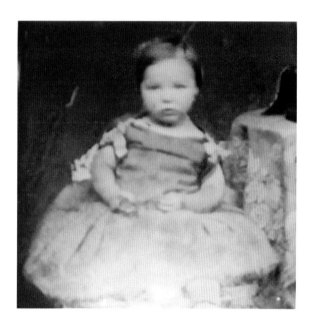

William Woodhouse in 1859 aged two years.
Private collection

William Woodhouse's father was a fisherman, as were his uncles. He would have witnessed from early childhood the hardships of being fishermen, to make a living to feed their families whilst being in competition with each other. The constant battle with the elements for survival, and the reliance on the Morecambe Bay tides. No doubt Woodhouse remembered these early days when he later painted the men of the bay going about their daily work.

By 1861 William Woodhouse, his parents and elder sisters, Mary and Elizabeth and younger sister Emily had left their fisherman's cottage in Morecambe Street and moved to a newer and larger house on Queens Terrace which overlooked the sea and was close to the shore. His mother, Hannah was letting rooms as an effective way to supplement their income. The holiday trade helped with their finances and therefore the status of the family. It was at Queens Terrace in 1862 that the family welcomed its final member, when Woodhouse's younger brother Alfred was born. It was probably around this time too that Woodhouse first showed artistic tendencies, when he was caught scratching pictures of birds on his desk with a pin whilst at Sunday school!

William Woodhouse was educated at the National School, Church Street, Poulton, where Robert Dugdale was the master. Lessons were fairly basic but it was here that his aptitude for drawing was recognized and he would be asked to draw on the blackboard, allowing his fellow pupils to copy his work. Realizing he had a talent for sketching and encouraged by his peers, Woodhouse decided to attend art classes at the Mechanics Institute, Lancaster, where the Storey Institute now stands.

From around 1871, under the tuition of Herbert Gilbert, Woodhouse proved to be an enthusiastic student. He frequently walked between Morecambe and Lancaster on dark, cold evenings to attend the classes, which comprised Life Drawing, Sketching and Modelling. Woodhouse studied hard for a number of years and consistently passed all his art examinations, and won prizes and certificates for his artwork. Even after the death of his father in 1874, Woodhouse persevered with his studies, although effectively he had become 'the man of the house' at the age of seventeen. It must have been very satisfying for Woodhouse, when in 1879, his art master reported that he was among the principal prizewinners at the Institute with the potential to become a successful artist: these achievements were used to set an example to the other students.

By 1881 Woodhouse had exhibited some of his work and had just started to establish himself as an artist; even so he continued as a student at the Institute because it was noted in 1883 that he had won a £5 prize in the 'Life Drawing' class. There were two other notable awards received by Woodhouse during his student days and worthy of a mention, both were given for oil paintings. One was entitled 'A Copy of a Head' by Sir Thomas Lawrence[1] and the second for 'A Landscape with Cattle' by Nicolaas Berchem.[2] These paintings were important pieces of work as they were used to challenge students to follow a master's technique.

As Woodhouse's passion for painting animals grew along with his reputation as an artist, he rented a small shop with a large window in Queen Street, just around the corner from Queens Terrace where he still lived with his mother, sister Emily and Alfred. This 'studio' was close to the blacksmiths where Woodhouse spent many hours both studying and sketching all aspects of the horse's anatomy. He also made visits to the knacker's yard where he would sometimes partake in a more detailed analysis of the animal!

It did not take long for Woodhouse's painting skills to come to the notice of the Gorton family. Perhaps because of their interest in the arts Woodhouse was soon ensconced in a studio, which was almost certainly rented from them. It stood on the corner of Edward Street and Market Street opposite the old gas works. At that time the gas works were managed by William Duff and later by his son James Robertson Duff, whose sister Ellen Hogarth was the subject of one of William Woodhouse's portraits.

CERTIFIED COPY OF AN ENTRY OF BIRTH

GIVEN AT THE GENERAL REGISTER OFFICE

Application Number R414457

REGISTRATION DISTRICT **Lancaster**

1857. BIRTH in the Sub-district of **Heaton** in the **County of Lancaster**

Columns:-	1	2	3	4	5	6	7	8	9	10
No.	When and where born	Name, if any	Sex	Name and surname of father	Name, surname and maiden surname of mother	Occupation of father	Signature, description and residence of informant	When registered	Signature of registrar	Name entered after registration
368	First October 1857 Morecambe Street Poulton	William	Boy	James Woodhouse	Hannah Woodhouse formerly Brookes	Fisher-man	Hannah Woodhouse Mother Morecambe Street Poulton	Fifth November 1857	James Bell Registrar	

CERTIFIED to be a true copy of an entry in the certified copy of a Register of Births in the District above mentioned.

Given at the GENERAL REGISTER OFFICE, under the Seal of the said Office, the .... **11th** .... day of .... **October** **2002**

BXBZ 660755

CAUTION: THERE ARE OFFENCES RELATING TO FALSIFYING OR ALTERING A CERTIFICATE AND USING OR POSSESSING A FALSE CERTIFICATE ©CROWN COPYRIGHT

WARNING: A CERTIFICATE IS NOT EVIDENCE OF IDENTITY.

BXBZ Series Dd 0770 3331 04/02 SPSL

Copy of the Birth Certificate of William Woodhouse

Office for National Statistics

17

Queens Terrace, (the row of houses on the left hand side of the photograph).
William Woodhouse lived here circa 1861, and sketched many scenes of the old harbour and
shoreline from the house.
Courtesy of Lancashire County Library North Division Morecambe Library & Information Service

A Working Sketch.   Pencil.
Courtesy of Lancaster City Museums

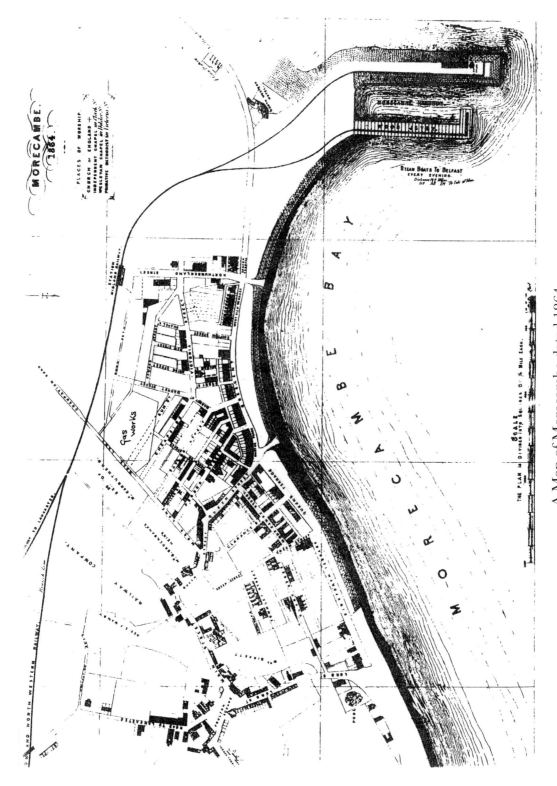

A Map of Morecambe dated 1864

Courtesy of Lancashire County Library North Division Morecambe Library & Information Service

The old Morecambe Gas Works, when William Duff was the Manager.
William Woodhouse's studio, at the corner of Edward Street and Market Street
would have overlooked these gas works.
Private collection

1889 was to be a memorable year for William Woodhouse. Firstly, he made a trip with two friends to the Near East and gathered a wealth of material, which he later included in some splendid paintings of his time abroad. Secondly, his ship S.S. Lizzie English called at Bremerhaven in Germany, where Woodhouse learnt that his painting entitled 'Doomed' had been accepted by the Royal Academy for inclusion in their forthcoming exhibition.

On the 1891 census return Woodhouse was described as 'Sculptor, Artist', however sculpture was not to play a significant part in Woodhouse's art career. As far as is known, the only signed piece of sculpture he made was of a bison. He had moved to 42 Green Street with his mother, Alfred and Elizabeth: however this was not to be his address for long as in 1892 he married Maria Emsley.

Maria Elizabeth Emsley was born on 9th June 1865 at Hartlington, Nr. Skipton, Yorkshire, and was the eldest child of Alfred Emsley, a farmer, and his wife Sarah nee Wilkins.

Maria was baptized on 19th November 1865 at the Parish Church of Burnsall and spent her childhood on her father's farm with her two sisters and four brothers who were born between 1866 and 1877. Maria was educated at a convent in Skipton before moving to Morecambe.

The 1881 census return showed that Alfred, who now worked as a commercial traveller, had moved his family to 3 Springfield Terrace. This was reported to have been one of the first four houses built in the West End of Morecambe. Alfred died in 1883, when Maria was seventeen years old and the family moved to 12 Yorkshire Street, where Maria with her mother and sister Edith were listed as 'confectioners' on the 1891 census return.

William Woodhouse and Maria Elizabeth Emsley married on 14th November 1892 at St. John's Church, Waterloo, Liverpool.

William Woodhouse and his wife, Maria Elizabeth, in the artist's Morecambe studio, 1890's
Courtesy of Lancaster City Museums

CERTIFIED COPY OF AN ENTRY OF MARRIAGE

GIVEN AT THE GENERAL REGISTER OFFICE

Application Number R414457

18 92 Marriage solemnized at ~ John Church in the Parish of Upton Warren in the County of Lancaster

No.	When Married	Name and Surname	Age	Condition	Rank or Profession	Residence at the time of Marriage	Father's Name and Surname	Rank or Profession of Father
90	November 14th 1892	William Woodhouse	36	Bachelor	Artist	North Road Waterloo	James Woodhouse (deceased)	Gentleman
		Maria Elizabeth Emsley	26	Spinster	—	North Road Waterloo	Alfred Emsley (deceased)	Mariner

Married in the Parish Church according to the Rites and Ceremonies of the Established Church, by Licence or after ___ by us,

This Marriage was solemnized between us, { William Woodhouse / Maria Elizabeth Emsley } in the Presence of us, { Roger Emsley / Nigel Woodhouse } / Elizabeth Jones

CERTIFIED to be a true copy of an entry in the certified copy of a register of Marriages in the Registration District of **West Derby**

Given at the GENERAL REGISTER OFFICE, under the Seal of the said Office, the **11th** day of **October** **2002**

MXB 132678

This certificate is issued in pursuance of section 65 of the Marriage Act 1949. Sub-section 3 of that section provides that any certified copy of an entry purporting to be sealed or stamped with the seal of the General Register Office shall be received as evidence of the marriage to which it relates without any further or other proof of the entry, and no certified copy purporting to have been given in the said Office shall be of any force or effect unless it is sealed or stamped as aforesaid.

CAUTION: THERE ARE OFFENCES RELATING TO FALSIFYING OR ALTERING A CERTIFICATE AND USING OR POSSESSING A FALSE CERTIFICATE. ©CROWN COPYRIGHT

01944J 3662 03/02 S*SL 002831

WARNING: A CERTIFICATE IS NOT EVIDENCE OF IDENTITY.

Copy of the Marriage Certificate of William Woodhouse & Maria Emsley

Office for National Statistics

In 1891-92 Woodhouse designed a house, which was built in Chatsworth Road and named Kenilcote. It was a most desirable area of Morecambe in which to live, as the house was in a rural position and looked out onto cornfields. The painting of 'The Reaper - Harvesting' shows Kenilcote in the background. Woodhouse also had a studio here at the far end of the garden where the walls were adorned with trophies of his hunting expeditions and other artist's accessories.

Sketches showing preparation work for
The Reaper – Harvesting. Pencil.
Courtesy of Lancaster City Museums

The Reaper - Harvesting.   Oil.
Courtesy of Lancaster City Museums

Kenilcote – taken in the snow. In the right background is a glimpse of the former Summer Gardens built in 1878. It was sold in 1898 and demolished when the area was developed for housing.

Private collection

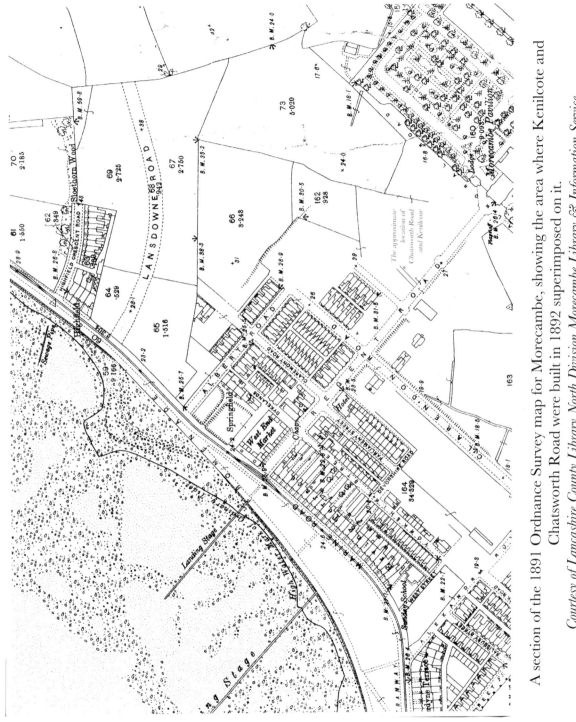

A section of the 1891 Ordnance Survey map for Morecambe, showing the area where Kenilcote and Chatsworth Road were built in 1892 superimposed on it.

Courtesy of Lancashire County Library North Division Morecambe Library & Information Service

William and Maria Woodhouse lived at Kenilcote following their marriage and their three children were born there:

| Harold Emsley Woodhouse | Born | 6th | January | 1894 |
| | Died | 18th | April | 1894 |

Harold was just over three months old when he died at Maria's sister's house in Ormskirk, he is buried at Morecambe Old Cemetery in a family grave.

| Marie Winifred Woodhouse (Winnie) | Born | 13th | April | 1895 |
| | Died | 17th | April | 1996 |

| Ronald Basil Emsley Woodhouse (Roy) | Born | 1st | July | 1897 |
| | Died | 16th | June | 1987 |

William Woodhouse was something of a Victorian father, and left the upbringing of his children to his wife Maria. Although he was a kindly man he was perhaps a little too preoccupied with his art, and did not spend much time with them during their childhood. However this did not affect his relationship with his family; he was always much revered and admired by them.

By the beginning of the 1900's, Chatsworth Road had been invaded by the expanding population of Morecambe. Although they still lived at Kenilcote at the time of the 1901 census return, the family moved in 1902 to a house on Furness Road, Heysham, which Woodhouse called 'Auburn Court'. Once again he had the peace and quiet he craved and a studio with north-facing light. The house was situated within easy walking distance of the shore and close to Heysham village, two areas where Woodhouse loved to sketch and paint.

Auburn Court with St John's Church.

Early 1900's Watercolour.

Courtesy of Lancaster City Museums

Interior of Kenilcote – Home of William Woodhouse and family.
Circa 1892 – 1902
Courtesy of Lancaster City Museums

At both Kenilcote and Auburn Court there were pieces of furniture, which had been carved by Woodhouse including cupboards, tables and a very large sideboard which featured a hunting scene. Also among his possessions was a small table with a brass plate inscribed 'Wm. Woodhouse': it is said that the wood for the table came from the original parish church of Poulton-le-Sands, which was demolished circa 1840. The plate was originally on the 'Woodhouse family pew' and referred to Woodhouse's grandfather.

Woodhouse also obtained an unusual bed head, which came from a liner that was broken up at Wards Ship Breakers Yard during the early 1900s. It was circular in shape and Woodhouse decorated it with a painting of flowers, which complimented a pretty frieze he had painted in one of the bedrooms.

Most of this furniture and bed head are held in the Lancaster City Museums 'Woodhouse collection'.

A photograph showing a sample of William Woodhouse's carving.
Private collection

The Bed head, which was decorated with flowers and birds by William Woodhouse.
Private collection image courtesy of Lancaster City Museums

Family photograph taken early 1900's
Left to Right Winnie Woodhouse, Sarah Emsley, (Maria's mother)
Maria Woodhouse and Roy Woodhouse.
Courtesy of Lancaster City Museums

William Woodhouse in his studio circa 1910
Courtesy of Lancaster City Museums

The painting on the easel is of his daughter Winnie dressed as "Little Red Riding Hood" accompanied by "The Big Bad Wolf".

Maria was well known in Morecambe for her extreme kindness, generosity and sweetness. Visitors to the house would always receive a warm welcome. When she died on 12th October 1925 after a long illness aged 60 years old, not only was her death keenly felt by Woodhouse, Winnie and Roy but by her wide circle of friends too. Maria's funeral service was held at St. Peter's Church, Heysham.

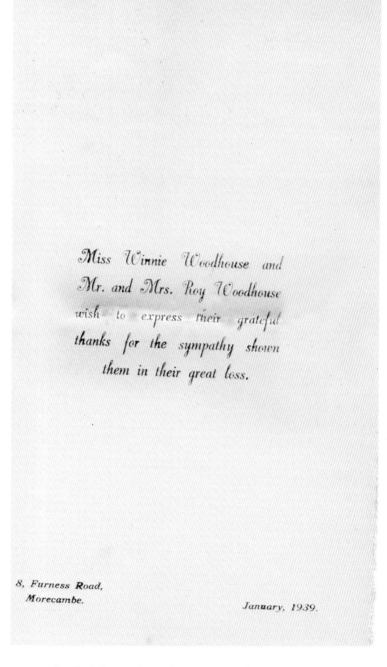

Miss Winnie Woodhouse and Mr. and Mrs. Roy Woodhouse wish to express their grateful thanks for the sympathy shown them in their great loss.

8, Furness Road, Morecambe.

January, 1939.

An In Memoriam Card for William Woodhouse.
Courtesy of Lancaster City Museums

Woodhouse lived for another thirteen years after Maria's death and with his daughter Winnie to keep house for him he remained at Auburn Court. He continued to paint and exhibit his work until he died quite suddenly on 13th January 1939, having been ill for only a few days. He was 81 years old. Woodhouse's funeral service was well attended and also took place at St. Peter's Church, where he and Maria are interred together in the churchyard.

After William Woodhouse's death many tributes were paid to him, one was written by my Great Uncle Dr. Christopher W. Hogarth and was published in the "Morecambe Visitor", 18th January 1939.

"Morecambe has grown so large since William Woodhouse and the writer were boys together and the artist was almost painfully shy and did not relish interruption whilst at work, that I imagine few knew what kind of man has passed from their midst and his worth as an artist. I knew him from boyhood until I last saw him in his studio three years ago.

Most public galleries throughout the kingdom have bought some of his works. I think it safe to say that no artist's work has been more reproduced and much of it in the most up-to-date methods, black and white, and in colour-processes, except maybe those given away with Christmas numbers.

When I first knew that he had chosen the life of an artist he had a small shop with a large glass window in Queen Street, which faced a Smithy, where many animals were shod, and he used to make studies of them whilst standing in his room — call it studio if you like, but here he did really good work and learned to sketch with a sureness and rapidity I have seldom seen equalled.

Then he moved to a larger place near the gasworks and afterwards to the house where he died, where he had a proper studio — north light, draw curtains etc., and if you approached it by the back entrance you would wonder who on earth could live there because on the walls of the garden were skulls and horns of many animals.

His best work always seemed to me that done in the district in which he lived and knew best, particularly Heysham when it was a village of one or two streets, and no sea-wall, with a few houses, from which on a still day the thin smoke from peat fires went straight up to the clouds.

No modern "improvements", no harbour, much the same condition in which the great artist Turner must have seen it when he made his drawing of the seashore there, except that in Turner's day there was more sand, the water was further away.

Sleep well; at least some of us in it, are happier for your work and the knowledge that we knew you in the flesh"!

Notes

No.1.   Sir Thomas Lawrence (1769 –1830) was a British artist who gained a reputation as a society painter in the late eighteenth and early nineteenth centuries. In 1792 he was appointed principal portrait painter to George III.

No 2.   Nicolaas Berchem (Circa 1620-1683) was a seventeenth century Dutch painter who was one of the most prolific of the Dutch masters. He painted landscapes as well as hunting scenes.

William and Maria Woodhouse's Headstone
St Peter's Churchyard, Heysham.

A Loving Memory

Maria Elizabeth
Woodhouse
1865 – 1925

William Woodhouse
1857 – 1939

Also their daughter

Marie Winifred
Woodhouse
1895 - 1996

Auburn Court, Furness Road, Heysham, Lancashire.

Auburn Court was the home of William and Maria Woodhouse and their family from 1902. After Maria and William died, Winnie remained at Auburn Court until her death in 1996.

Private Collection (Photograph taken 1996)

William Woodhouse
The young artist.

Courtesy of Lancaster City Museums

A Self Portrait showing William Woodhouse surrounded by the animals
he so loved to sketch and paint. Pencil drawing.
Courtesy of Lancaster City Museums

CHAPTER 2

WILLIAM WOODHOUSE – A Glimpse at the Artist.

William Woodhouse is probably best known as an animal painter who had a love for all creatures great and small. He excelled at painting horses and dogs, but is remembered too for his bird paintings, land and seascapes, and his portraits, although most of these were of his family. As a young artist Woodhouse was painting at a time when the Landseer School of Painting was popular. Although he may have been inspired by the artist's great animal paintings, Woodhouse did not try to emulate Landseer as he was already beginning to find success using his own style and techniques.

Woodhouse was a perfectionist, and one of his greatest strengths was in his preparation work. Topics for his paintings were always researched with great care, and he had a wonderful eye for detail. His numerous pencil drawings, with their simplicity of line were Woodhouse's trademark, and show how much work went into composing a picture. With infinite patience he would sketch every aspect of his subjects, never stopping until he was satisfied he had mastered all the finer points. Only then would he embark on the final painting. A harness for a horse, an old plough, the inside of a blacksmith's forge or the rigging on a ship, they all had to be correct, which is why some of Woodhouse's paintings are so important today. They meticulously record a bygone era.

Chillingham Cattle. Oil.
Courtesy of Lancaster City Museums

Most of Woodhouse's earlier paintings were in oils. He rediscovered for himself a technique once used by Rubens, which was to prime his canvases with a silver grey coating which he then allowed to show through various parts of the painting, giving a depth and quality to a picture not always easily accomplished using oils. Woodhouse also often used pure, vibrant colours making his work bold and assured. This combined with his talent for applying both light and shade, created volume, texture and movement, and gave his work a most life-like and harmonious quality.

Animals played a large part in Woodhouse's early works, and exhibition pieces during the 1880's and 1890's often featured wild animals, dogs, horses and cattle. Although many of these cattle came from the herds that roamed around the Lune Estuary or the Highlands of Scotland, some were Chillingham cattle from Chillingham Park in Northumberland. A painting of these unique beasts, which are the only pure bred cattle not to have been crossed with the domestic cow earned Woodhouse much praise.

A number of oil paintings which became well known, including Woodhouse's Royal Academy exhibits, were of bison, buffalo and wolves from Canada, as well as moose and wapiti (North American Elks). His settings on the Canadian Prairies, in the woods, or around the lakes of their homeland could not be faulted for their accuracy. Woodhouse created the most realistic scenes from countries he had not visited personally. He never travelled to either Canada or America, which make these works all the more remarkable. While a few of these paintings portray poise and tranquillity within the animal kingdom, most pictures depict great animal battles and struggles for survival and supremacy. Woodhouse repeatedly appeared to capture not only the character of the animals but their moods and spirit too.

At times Woodhouse must have felt handicapped living so far away from a zoo or natural history museum. In 1891 he visited the Zoological Gardens in London where he had the opportunity to observe, sketch and paint at close quarters the animals found in both Great Britain and foreign parts.

Ticket for admittance to the
Zoological Society
of London Gardens 1891

Courtesy of Lancaster City Museums

Woodhouse was very fond of painting dogs, and he was rarely without 'a faithful companion' at his side. There are many pencil drawings and sketches of his family pets, made as they all relaxed happily at home. In 1889 a local Westmorland newspaper reported that Woodhouse had painted a picture entitled 'Bobby and the Kendal Hounds'. It quoted that *"Mr. Woodhouse's dogs were capital portraits, full of character, and the grouping very spirited and natural and each dog was so recognizable that it could be identified by its name"*. It should be mentioned that Woodhouse only painted dogs that were known to him and never invented a fictitious one for inclusion in any of his paintings.

It is widely acknowledged that some of Woodhouse's greatest works were his sporting pictures of dogs and game. These paintings often included his two gun dogs, named Jess and Turk, the dark colours of his handsome setter Jess, contrasting beautifully with those of his white and tan dog Turk. Woodhouse was a very good shot, and at times he found it hard to decide whether to use his gun or his paintbrush! Perhaps one of the reasons why he took part in shooting expeditions, on the moors of Lancashire, Yorkshire and Scotland were so that the contents of his bag could be used extensively in his sporting pictures. William Pape, a master gun maker from Northumberland renowned for his double-barrelled shotgun, used a few of these paintings for advertising purposes, which benefited Woodhouse as it indirectly publicized his work too.

The Faithful Trio.
Oil. Private collection, USA
Courtesy of Burlington Paintings London

William Woodhouse had a meticulous eye for detail and he would study and sketch subjects before embarking on a final picture. Pencil sketches.
Courtesy of Lancaster City Museums

One of Woodhouse's paintings entitled 'The Taxidermist' gives a good indication of the rewards achieved from his shooting forays. It shows George Mussell, the taxidermist pursuing his craft, which enabled Woodhouse to cram his studio with stuffed birds, animal heads and other shooting trophies! We may think this rather gruesome today, but it was very acceptable in Victorian times. Woodhouse, like other artists of the period was sometimes forced to use lifeless specimens. These paintings reflect his caring and sympathetic empathy for all creatures. He had the ability to compose pictures which made the animals and birds appear to be very much alive, and devoid of any unnatural stiffness or poses. This result was achieved by many hours spent recording and sketching all the wildlife he encountered on his numerous field trips coupled with his deep anatomical knowledge.

The Taxidermist – George Mussell (1827 – 1909)
surrounded by examples of his work. Oil.
Courtesy of Lancaster City Museums

The landed gentry were keen to commission Woodhouse to paint pictures for them representing their sporting pursuits, not only on grouse and pheasant shoots but on the hunting field too, where the thrill of the chase was paramount.

A Hunting Scene. Watercolour.
Private collection

Woodhouse's versatility as an artist equipped him with the necessary flair to capture the majesty of a stag at bay, or the baying of the hounds as 'hunted and hunter' vied for dominance. He travelled to several parts of the British Isles and it was not unknown for him to spend time at a Country Estate painting his Lordship's favourite hunter, polo pony or other animals in the stable. On these occasions I'm sure, the animals attracted him much more than the human beings, and he probably enjoyed painting them more than he did their owners and grooms! Woodhouse made many visits to see family and friends who lived in and around the Skipton area of Yorkshire, and to Banbury in Oxfordshire. Never without a pencil and paper, Woodhouse sketched and painted prolifically within the towns and surrounding countryside. He also enjoyed trips to the East Coast of England, around the Staithes and Redcar area. Woodhouse sailed to the Isle of Man and to the Western Isles of Scotland: he always enjoyed these voyages by sea, often travelling with companions. He spent time on the Farne Islands where he encountered the might of the sea, and the majesty of the sea going birds. Some of his exhibits, which appeared at the Harris Museum and Art Gallery exhibitions featured the Pinnacles and birds from these islands, including kittiwakes and gannets. It was probably whilst visiting these islands that Woodhouse also visited Bamburgh

Castle, which is close by and painted the castle from the shore. It is known that he also visited Bruges in Belguim as there are various sketches as well as paintings from around the town, although the exact date of this trip is not known.

Bamburgh Castle. Oil.
Home of the Armstrong family.
Private collection

While Woodhouse may have painted many game birds, he was equally happy to be found on the seashore observing and sketching the wading birds. From a rock opposite the site where the Grosvenor Hotel once stood, close to Sandylands Promenade, Morecambe, Woodhouse spent many happy hours watching the cormorants. He was also very adept at painting the birds of the countryside happily engaged in their everyday life, be it scratching around for food, swimming lazily on a pond, preening their feathers or just simply idling the day away.

Woodhouse painted 'Morecambe people at work', the fishermen with their horses and carts shrimping on the shoreline, and the mussel-gatherers on the skeers. He painted the donkeys on the beach with their boys waiting patiently to give rides to the holiday makers. He painted horses at the tram depot or at the blacksmith's forge, and during the First World War in their army stables. He painted ships stranded on the sands at low tide or on their way to Wards Breakers Yard, which was where the jetty now stands. When a circus had come to town Woodhouse was sure to have been there, having taken the opportunity to sketch and paint the animals and circus folk, as he had when he visited a Wild West Show at The Belle Vue, Manchester. This gave him the inspiration for his painting of 'Buffalo Bill'.

Buffalo Bill. Watercolour.
Courtesy of Lancaster City Museums
The first time Buffalo Bill brought his Wild West Show to Britain was in 1887 to help celebrate Queen Victoria's Jubilee, his last visit was in 1904.

In the early days William Woodhouse relied on his family and friends to buy his work. His brother Alfred, a painter and decorator, loyally supported him and found him commissions from among his customers. My late father could remember William visiting his parents house for supper, and my grandfather buying the odd painting "to help Willie out" in the days when he was striving to gain recognition as an accomplished artist! Eventually, some of his more popular works, especially the animal paintings were reproduced, firstly by Storey Brothers and Co. Ltd. of Lancaster, one of the earliest firms to reproduce paintings and then by The Fine Arts Publishing Company of London. This made Woodhouse's work more accessible and familiar to the general public.

Painting for Woodhouse was both a living and a hobby, and after the First World War when it became more fashionable he painted in watercolour. Woodhouse's watercolours were more muted in colour than his oil paintings, and he sometimes used a stippling technique, favoured by some of the French artists. Landscape painting had long been a British art tradition. Increasingly, rural nostalgia with glimpses of country life became a popular form of art. Woodhouse painted farms and farmyards and beauty spots such as Silverdale and Sunderland Point. He painted country lanes and village ponds and various scenes around Morecambe Bay from the land and the shore. These sentimental and pretty pictures were always in demand and were snapped up by visitors and residents alike, and in his world were the more commercial side of his trade. Woodhouse was often observed walking locally. He walked to all his painting sites, and was not discouraged by the length of a journey even when after a day's work he had to walk back home again carrying his artist's material. On one occasion he walked to Bailrigg on the south side of Lancaster, approximately five miles from his studio to paint a donkey with a very long tail, which belonged to the Storey boys. He was understandably very tired when he arrived back home, but he loved the outdoor life and was never happier than when he could study his subjects in their natural surroundings.

Silverdale
from the Shore.
Watercolour.
Private collection

For many years as Woodhouse sketched and painted locally, he watched and recorded Morecambe growing and flourishing. The changes he witnessed were plentiful, making his paintings of historical value, as they record Morecambe as it was before and after The First World War, and before it was lost to the developers. Even today old buildings and familiar historical parts of Morecambe, which appeared in his paintings, are being pulled down and vanishing under the guise of progress. Woodhouse certainly lived during a time of great progress, but he was not so interested in his 'modern day' Morecambe, where horses, one of his favourite subjects gave way to cars and motor driven trams. His memories of the old days never dimmed, and just before his death in 1939 he was at his easel completing a painting of a blacksmith at work, having only days before complained to his brother "that the days were too short and the light faded all too quickly". Sadly this was to be his final work.

The Blacksmith. Watercolour.
The last painting to be completed by William Woodhouse.
Private collection

After Woodhouse's death, his family sent over one hundred paintings to A.L. Price's shop[1] at Lancaster to be sold. This allowed friends, and admirers of his work a final opportunity to purchase one of his pictures before they all disappeared into private collections.

The family also presented an oil painting of 'a teal', which was painted in 1886, to Morecambe Bay Wildfowling Club, which is now known as the Morecambe Bay Wildfowlers Association. Woodhouse had been an active Vice President and life member of the club. The painting was framed, inscribed and hung at the Golden Ball Public House, Heaton with Oxcliffe where committee meetings were held. Eventually the painting was loaned to the British Association for Shooting and Conservation where it was hung in the library at their headquarters, Marford Mill, Rossett, Wrexham. In 1992 a further oil painting, 'study of teal' dated 1888 was purchased by the Morecambe Bay Wildfowlers Association, and was presented on loan to the British Association for Shooting and Conservation, Northern Region, and hung, where it can be admired by visitors to their offices at Gisburn, Lancashire.

A revival of interest in Woodhouse's work took place some forty years after he died, when his paintings were once again collected in earnest. Although today his pictures do not command such high prices as the heady days of the 1980's and 1990's they are still highly prized, loved by their owners, and sought after by those who appreciate his work. Woodhouse's work continues to appear at private and public galleries, and at auctions around the British Isles as well as overseas.

Many friends would have had fond memories of Woodhouse and plenty of interesting tales to tell, therefore it is pleasing that at least one anecdote has survived over the years, and refers to one of his painting's entitled **'The Fodder Gang'**. A picture covered in grime and looking very much the worse for wear appeared for sale at a local secondhand shop where it was described as 'an old master'. Several of Woodhouse's friends saw the painting and were convinced it was one of his pictures, so they persuaded him to visit the shop to see the work for himself. One can only imagine his surprise and amusement when he found that it was indeed his painting of The Fodder Gang, which was being passed off as 'an old master'. No doubt Woodhouse had a few words with the dealer about misleading his customers, and a good chuckle with his friends about it afterwards.

Woodhouse related this tale to friends at an exhibition held at the Harris Art Gallery in 1927 when a reproduction of his painting 'The Fodder Gang' was on display.

Notes

No.1   A.L. Price's shop. Alfred Price, a carver, gilder and picture frame maker started a picture framing business circa 1885, and Woodhouse sent some of his paintings to the shop to be framed. Alfred's son, William, worked for his father and as the business grew they restored, cleaned and varnished paintings and opened a gallery where they sold paintings. William Price took over from Alfred when he died in 1928. Both men were highly respected within the art world, and enjoyed a long and happy association with Woodhouse. Firstly as picture framers and secondly by selling some of his work in their gallery.

The Mechanics Institute, Lancaster where
William Woodhouse attended Art Classes.
Courtesy of Lancaster Reference Library

The Institute was founded in 1824. Its library opened a year later followed by educational classes, which were introduced during the 1840's. By 1856 the Mechanics Institute was situated in Market Street where it remained until the opening of the Storey Institute.

The Storey Institute Lancaster.
Courtesy of Lancaster Reference Library

In 1887 when Thomas Storey (1825-1898) was Mayor of Lancaster, he decided to mark Queen Victoria's Jubilee with a grand gesture. He gave the town the Storey Institute which cost him £20,000. It was given to further the cause of technical and art education in Lancaster. It also provided an art gallery, additional classrooms and a public library. The new building which incorporated the Mechanics Institute and was built on it's site opened in 1891. Woodhouse's paintings were exhibited at the gallery on many occasions.

All the Storey family were the most generous of benefactors who took a great interest in supporting the town. They were also ardent educationalists.

William Woodhouse.   Oil.
Private collection image Courtesy of Lancaster City Museums

CHAPTER 3

WILLIAM WOODHOUSE - Paintings.

Woodhouse was a prolific painter whose work covered a variety of topics. The majority of his paintings were for sale, although he kept some of his pictures to use as examples of his work, or as family pieces. Some paintings were not for public display as they were privately commissioned. Today his work can be seen at public art galleries and museums although most of his paintings are still in private ownership.

The following chapter is designed to show as many different aspects of Woodhouses's work as possible, and to observe his skill at recording accurately all that he saw around him. Woodhouse usually signed his paintings and gave them titles, but only a few were dated.

As Woodhouse loved to sketch and paint animals and birds at work, rest and play, it is fitting to start with a selection of animal paintings.

All Creatures Great and Small – let the animals 'do the talking'!

Tiger.   Oil.
Private collection image courtesy of Lancaster City Museums

Polar Bear with Cubs.   Oil.
Courtesy of Lancaster City Museums

Hares.   Watercolour.
Private collection image courtesy of Lancaster City Museums

Monarch of the Glen.   Oil.
Courtesy of Lancaster City Museums

Orvar of the Holm.   Oil.
Private collection

Orvar, an Elkhound born in 1928 was a mature dog when acquired by William Woodhouse. He was sent by rail from Middlesex to Silverdale in Cumbria, and Winnie could remember receiving a telephone call from the station informing them of Orvar's arrival.   Orvar was devoted to his master, although sadly after Woodhouse's death his temperament changed and it became necessary to have him put to sleep.   He was wrapped in Roy's army greatcoat and buried in the grounds of a house close to Auburn.

Elkhounds were imported into this country from Norway, possibly by an artist acquaintance of the Prince of Wales, later King Edward VII.

It is interesting to notice William's eye for detail once again, with the inclusion of snowshoes in the painting.

Birds

When Woodhouse painted birds the surroundings had to satisfy the eye as much as the bird portraiture. Winter plumage had to be accompanied by winter scenes, the leafless trees, the frozen pond or the frosty dawn, just as summer plumage had to be accompanied by sunny scenes. He also took into account the colour changes in the feathers between the adult, juvenile and immature birds. While some changes were subtle others were more defined. Woodhouse's bird paintings are a fine example of a man devoted to the study and observation of his 'feathered friends'.

Cormorant and Chicks, Mona's Isle. Oil.
Private collection image courtesy of Lancaster City Museums

Eagle and Prey.   Watercolour.
Private collection image courtesy of Lancaster City Museums

Snipe & Teal.   Watercolour.
Private collection

Lapwings.   Watercolour.
Courtesy of Harris Museum and Art Gallery, Preston, Lancashire.

Lapwings are a common sight around Morecambe Bay. This painting was purchased after the Memorial Exhibition of 1939, which was held at the Harris Museum and Art Gallery.

After the Duck Shoot.   Watercolour.
Private collection

Boats and Ships

When Woodhouse lived in a house overlooking the seashore and harbour he watched and sketched many different kinds of boats as they sailed in with the tide. Sometimes he would see a boat stranded at low water or wrecked when gales lashed the coast and with the arrival of Wards Ship Breakers Yard at Morecambe's stone jetty in 1905 came an interesting array of old hulks for Woodhouse to study.

Top and Middle: Brighton Terrace, Morecambe from the shore.
Bottom: A Nobby[1] Pencil.
Courtesy of Lancaster City Museums

Notes

No.1   A Nobby, meaning easy to handle and sail, is the local Lancashire name for these graceful looking boats. Built at Arnside, Cumbria from 1880, they are of carvel construction as the planks rest against each other as opposed to overlapping. Nobbies were used mainly for shrimping although they could be used as fishing boats. In their heyday these boats would be raced on regatta days, before sail gave way to power in 1924.

The Wreck of the Vanadis.   Watercolour sketch.
Courtesy of Lancaster City Museums

The Vanadis, a Norwegian barque, was badly damaged when she was blown ashore at Half Moon Bay, Heysham in 1903. Sailing under the Russian flag she was carrying a cargo of timber from Georgia, USA, to Fleetwood, which was rescued from the stricken vessel and taken ashore by horse and cart. The Vanadis was eventually broken up in the bay, and even today remains of the old wreck can be seen at low tide. Woodhouse and his son visited the wreck on several occasions and made watercolour sketches of the Vanadis at various stages of her break up.

HMS Northampton. Watercolour sketch.
Morecambe 1905
Courtesy of Lancaster City Museums

HMS Northampton was the first ship to enter Wards Ship Breakers Yard on September 30th 1905. She was an iron frigate, which had been built in 1876, and was sold to Wards for £15,800 for scrap. Messrs. Thomas Ward of Sheffield developed Morecambe Harbour as a ship breakers yard in 1905. It was situated where the jetty now stands and operated until 1931. Many ships were taken there to be broken up, and despite the dirt and noise it became a huge tourist attraction as well as giving employment to many local men. Woodhouse spent a considerable amount of time at the yard making sketches of the vessels which arrived there, including HMS Akbar, HMS Orlando and Raleigh, to name but a few.

HMS Akbar.   Watercolour.
Morecambe circa 1908
Courtesy of Lancaster City Museums

HMS Akbar was the oldest vessel to be broken up at Wards Ship Breakers Yard. She was built in 1816 and was formerly the 74-gun 'wooden wall' Wellington. For over forty years before she arrived at Wards in April 1908, HMS Akbar had served as a training vessel.

Donkeys

Seaside holidays meant donkey rides on the beach, which were always in demand with the holidaymakers. Woodhouse used to enjoy painting the donkeys and their boys on the sands at Morecambe, as they waited patiently for customers. Occasionally one of the boys was summoned to take the donkeys down to Woodhouse's house, and he would sit outside his front door and sketch them! Some of these paintings, due to their popularity, were later reproduced in the form of greeting cards.

Donkeys on the Beach. Oil.
Private collection

Donkey Boy. Oil. Painted 1925 / 1930
Given to Lancaster City Museum 1932 by William Woodhouse

Family Portraits and Paintings

Woodhouse painted very few portraits, and those he did were mostly of his family. He painted his wife Maria as a young woman, capturing her sweet and gentle nature. His daughter Winnie is featured in several paintings, often as a child posing with animals, birds and family pets. His son Roy is painted on the battlefield in 1916. (See First World War paintings).

Maria Elizabeth Woodhouse.   Oil.
Courtesy of Lancaster City Museums

This painting was presented to the Lancaster City Museum in 1981 as a gift from Roy and Winnie.

Marie Winifred (Winnie) as a young girl.
Oil. *Private collection*

Winnie as a young lady 1912.
Oil. *Courtesy of Lancaster City Museums*

Hannah Woodhouse, Williams mother.   Oil.
Private collection

Ellen Hogarth with her daughter Joan in 1904-5.   Oil.
Private collection

Ellen was the daughter of William Duff, manager of the Morecambe Gas Works circa1869-
1901.   Ellen married Dr. Bertram W. Hogarth JP who was affectionately known as 'The
Major' by fellow Morecambrians.   They had five children; the picture on the wall, to the right
of Joan, is of their eldest daughter Marjorie who died in infancy.

William Woodhouse could produce paintings from photographs, which he studied and then copied.

A photograph of my late father on his camel "Mut" taken during the Locust Campaign,
Palestine – 1930

A watercolour sketch by William Woodhouse copied from the above photograph; Woodhouse
was over seventy years old when he painted this picture.
Private collection

Farms and Farming

Woodhouse visited many farms around Morecambe and Heysham sketching and painting the farmhouses, outbuildings and farmyards. He went into the fields where he saw horses and ploughs tilling the land, and the agricultural labourers hard at work. He painted scenes at harvest time, and the animals as they nestled down beside the haystacks or quietly grazed nearby. He watched the farmer as he brought the cows in for milking, and sketched the cattle in their byre.

Moss House Farm.   Oil.
Private collection image courtesy of Lancaster City Museums

Moss House Farm was once the home of Titus Escolme, who was an acquaintance of Woodhouse. On the 1881 census return it was described as a 45acre farm, and Titus employed two farm labourers. He was unmarried and his niece Elizabeth Escolme was his housekeeper. By 1891 Titus had a new housekeeper and a domestic servant, he also continued to employ two farm labourers.

The gentleman in the painting is Titus Escolme with his dog bringing the cows home for milking.

A Barn at Moss House Farm.   Oil.
Private collection

Titus Escolme feeding his cattle.   Oil.
Courtesy of Lancaster City Museums

The First World War

The First World War years must have been a worrying and harrowing time for William, and his wife Maria, as their son Roy served in the Royal Garrison Artillery in France. Roy was badly injured at Etaples and spent many months in hospital, both abroad and in England. Whilst William continued to paint the scenes around Morecambe he could not have failed to see the changes that war inevitably brought. Although he did not appear to paint too many pictures showing the horror of the war recorded titles do testify to its influence on, or maybe inevitable intrusion into his work.

Works exhibited with a war theme:
Army Horses in their Stables
Crossing the Channel 1914
The Troop Ship
1914
Bringing up the Guns
Charging the Guns
The Last Cavalry Charge 1914 - (a pair of paintings)?
Cavalry Horses
Flanders Field
The Perils of War
The Lights of Peace

Army Horses in their Stables. Oil.
Courtesy of Lancaster City Museums

One of William's most poignant pictures is an oil painting of Roy, painted as a tribute to his gallant son. Roy is on the battlefield, and he has just fired a Howitzer gun, which shows correctly, that the lanyard is detached. This painting is a good example of William's eye for detail.

Roy Woodhouse, on the battlefield during the First World War. Oil.
Courtesy of Lancaster City Museums

This painting was donated to Lancaster City Museum by the family in 1987, and forms part of their Art Collection.

Horses

One of William's favourite topics when painting was definitely the horse. William loved horses and he always sketched and painted them with enjoyment and sympathy. His understanding and knowledge of them enabled him to portray their grace, spirit and beauty. Whether large or small, young or old, William would capture every fibre of their body, every straining muscle and distinguishing mark. Bridles, harnesses and saddles were always perfect in every detail as were the stables and their occupants.

Horses painted by William included:
Circus horses.
Horses on the shore at the water's edge, pulling carts containing mussels and shrimps.
Horses at the farriers
Horses belonging to friends
Horses pulling ploughs across the fields
Mares with their foals
Pack horses, seen on his Middle Eastern trip
Polo ponies
Railway horses
Tram horses
Wild horses and ponies of the moors

Stable Companions.   Oil.
Courtesy of Lancaster City Museums

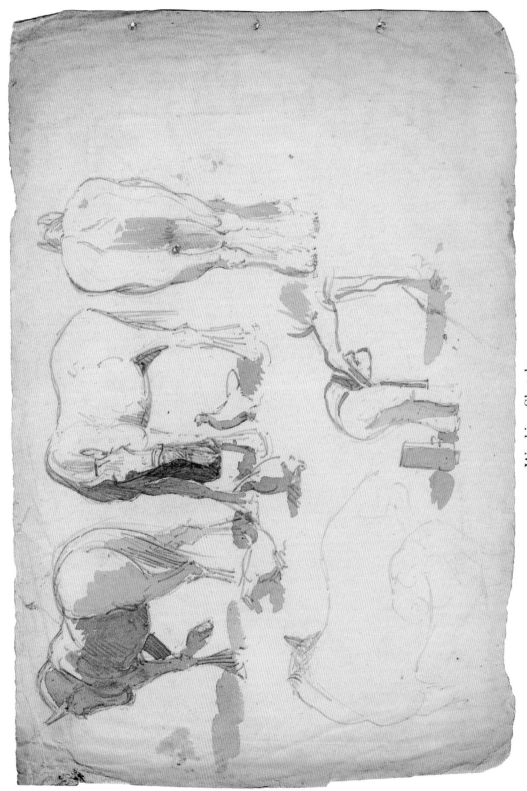

Working Sketches.
Courtesy of Lancaster City Museums

Study of a Horse.   Watercolour.

Horse and Foal.   Watercolour.
Courtesy of Harris Museum and Art Gallery, Preston, Lancashire

Both paintings were purchased after the Memorial Exhibition held at the Harris Art Gallery in 1939.

Majestic. Oil.
Courtesy of Lancaster City Museums

Majestic, the Blacker family's horse, an oil painting signed and dated 1909. When the Blacker family who were friends and neighbours of William Woodhouse moved house, the painting was too large to fit any of the walls, so it was donated to the Museum. Copies of this painting were published by the Lancaster City Museums in 1995 to mark the 100th birthday of the artist's daughter, Marie Winifred Woodhouse (Winnie).

Local Scenes

Woodhouse spent nearly all of his life working around Morecambe Bay and the surrounding area, and produced many paintings recording the landscape. The following titles represent just a few of these paintings, and are designed to bring to mind local scenes and a bygone era, which were part of Woodhouse's everyday life.

In line with popular nostalgia Woodhouse sometimes 'dressed' his landscapes and buildings with period figures – like the cavaliers he set at Borwick Hall. Such historical interest flourished after the likes of community pageants, which were staged in the first third of the twentieth century across Britain.

Borwick Hall in Olden Times
Brookhouse Village
The Canal at Hest Bank
Crossing the Lancaster Sands - Olden Times (this included a guide and outriders)
The Cumbrian Hills
The Donkey Boy
Fishermen
The Gleaners
Golden Ball, Snatchems
Heysham Baulks[1]
Heysham Old Hall
Heysham Village
Heysham in Winter
The Old Golf Links - Heysham
A Rocky Point - Heysham
The Shore - Heysham
The Village Pump - Heysham
The Horse Thresher
Lobster Fisher
Off to the Mussel Skeers[2]
Mussel Gatherers[2]
Mussel Carts[2]
Waiting for the Mussel Boats, Morecambe
Morecambe 70 Years ago - After an old drawing
The Lightship
Obsolete (Two old hulks waiting to be destroyed at Wards Ship Breakers Yard)
The Groom
The Shoeing Forge
The Smithy
St. Patrick's Chapel - Heysham
St. Patrick's Ruins - Heysham (My late great uncle Dr. Fred W. Hogarth, a local historian, wrote several articles about St. Patrick's Chapel and ruins).
The Stackyard

Sunderland Point

Sunset over Morecambe Bay

Wagon Horse, Old Jetty - Morecambe

Old Harbour - Morecambe (showing the cattle and pigs being unloaded from the steamers which brought them in from Ireland. My father as a boy, would watch the milkmaids in draughty sheds milking the cows as soon as they were ashore).

As some of Woodhouse's ancestors were fishermen it is quite possible that they used the baulks and gathered mussels to supplement their income or to feed their families, as well as the more conventional method of fishing from boats. They may have gone shrimping, walking along the Bay with nets or trawled using a shallow-draughted vessel, or as the painting of 'Shrimpers'[3] depicts they would have walked along the edge of the tide with a horse and cart. The cart having nets attached which would catch the shrimps.

Notes

No.1   Baulks were long V-shaped fences generally made of hazel. The apex of the V was placed into the water at a depth of seven feet. Fish would become trapped on an ebbing tide and pass through a narrow opening in the V and become caught in a net. Almost any size of fish could be caught this way.

No. 2   Skeers were large tracts of rough ground, parts of which were left uncovered by the ebb tide and where the mussel beds were to be found. The mussel gatherers raked up the mussels with long or short rakes called 'a craam' and shook them into baskets made of willow, either a horse and cart or a boat would ferry them ashore.

No. 3   The painting, which was entitled 'Shrimpers,' was bought by the Harris Museum and Art Gallery, Preston, Lancashire. See page 102)

The Mussel Gatherers.   Watercolour.
Courtesy of Lancaster City Museums

Cavaliers at Borwick Hall.   Watercolour.
Private collection image courtesy of Lancaster City Museums

Borwick Hall.   Watercolour.
Courtesy of Lancaster City Museums

The Canal at Hest Bank.   Watercolour.
Courtesy of Lancaster City Museums

Sunset over Morecambe Bay.   Watercolour.
Private collection image courtesy of Lancaster City Museums

Heysham Old Hall.   Watercolour.
Private collection

Heysham Old Hall was a beautiful Elizabethan Manor House built in 1598 with secret passages, priest holes and a hidden stairway leading to the attics. In 1857 Reverend John Royds, whose family were rectors in Heysham for over a hundred years bought the Hall. The last family occupant to live there was Miss Maggie Royds who became something of a recluse. After her death the Hall fell into disrepair and was saved from dereliction by William Barker, a brewer from Lancaster. Today it is a Public House.

Winnie, Roy and their friends played badminton at the Hall with members of the Royds family.

Heysham in Winter.   Watercolour.
Courtesy of Haworth Art Gallery, Accrington (Hyndburn Borough Council)

Shrimping.   Oil.
Courtesy of Lancaster City Museums

A Fisherman aboard the Wild Rose.   Oil.
Private collection image courtesy of Lancaster City Museums

CHAPTER 4

THE FINE ARTS PUBLISHING COMPANY

The Fine Arts Publishing Company of Green Street, London reproduced some of Woodhouse's oil paintings as prints. A catalogue produced by them unfortunately undated, lists the artist, the title of the work, and a very small illustration of the print. The outer cover of the catalogue states 'Beautiful Pictures For Home Decoration'. It is thought the catalogue, and Woodhouse's assocation with the company, dates from around 1915.

There was something to suit everyone's taste as the company had reproduced a wide range of subjects from Woodhouse's repertoire. It was more than likely that the commercial interests of the company rather than Woodhouse's will determined the range of images produced.

Card Titles:

Bison at Bay	
Black and White	(an English Setter with a Gordon Setter)
British Watch-dogs	(two cute puppies)!
Kittens	
The Morning meal	(Winnie, Woodhouse's daughter as a small girl feeding the birds)
A Muzzle is not always necessary	
The Performing Bear	
The Pigeons Bath	
The Poacher	
On the Sands: Morning	(both Morning and Evening are of donkeys on the sands
On the Sands: Evening	at Morecambe)
The Sea Birds Fortress	
Sportsman's Friend	(Setter and Game Bird)
Stag at Bay	
Stand Still	(A Horse at the Blacksmith's)

The records and offices of The Fine Arts Publishing Co. were destroyed during the Second World War.

A Muzzle is not always necessary.   Oil.
Courtesy of Lancaster City Museums

Performing Bear.   Oil.
Courtesy of Lancaster City Museums

CHAPTER 5

WILLIAM WOODHOUSE – The Great Adventure 1889.

Although Woodhouse liked the peaceful life around Morecambe Bay he was not a man without a sense of adventure, as the trip he took to the Near East shows.

At the end of March 1889 Woodhouse with two companions, Crockford and Nelson boarded the 'Moss Brow' at Cardiff, their destination – Constantinople.

Woodhouse, determined to make the most of his time away, had begun sketching soon after the boat had set sail. He also meticulously kept a diary, where he recorded details of the voyage. (See appendix I for a full transcript).

Woodhouse captured on paper all the wildlife and sights he encountered on the trip, this included the Channel Fleet and 'Trafalgar' before rounding the Rock of Gibraltar and sailing on to Port Said, where he enjoyed visiting the Arab markets and bazaars. He travelled up the Suez Canal to take part in a shooting expedition, and saw a Russian convict ship pass through the canal with convicts on board heading for Siberia.

After their arrival in Constantinople, which Woodhouse found overcrowded and noisy, the three friends disembarked from the Moss Brow and awaited the arrival of the S.S. Lizzie English from Russia, which was to bring them back to England. Due to fog in the Black Sea the ship was delayed so Woodhouse took a trip up the Bosphorus[1], which he found pretty and picturesque.

Before leaving Constantinople Woodhouse visited the crowded streets of Stamboul and made sketches of a Mosque. Having left port the Lizzie English sailed close to the land and Woodhouse observed camels and oxen pulling ploughs, and was intrigued to see that the horses and wagons had adopted the Russian harness.

Woodhouse was pleased to go ashore at Malta where he was able to speak English with the locals, before the boat sailed on to Gibraltar. Here she docked and took on 180 tons of coal, and Woodhouse attended a feast day on the Rock.

While crossing the Bay of Biscay Woodhouse had watched a whale, 'spouting water' before the ship was hit by atrocious weather conditions, her safety threatened. Woodhouse sustained a nasty thigh injury when he was thrown off balance in his cabin, so he must have been relieved when the ship passed the Channel Islands and the Isle of Wight. The captain had previously agreed to dock at Dover, to allow Woodhouse and his companions to disembark, but the continued bad weather conditions and light had made this impossible. So unperturbed they were forced to sail to Bremerhaven in Germany, the S.S. Lizzie English's final destination.

Before Woodhouse had left on his trip he had submitted a painting to the Royal Academy entitled 'Doomed', which he hoped would be accepted for their forthcoming exhibition. On his arrival at Bremerhaven he received a telegram from his brother-in-law Jack Warriner, which simply said 'Doomed accepted'. With what must have been extremely exciting news for Woodhouse he went ashore and the following day left for Southampton on the North German Lloyd Steamer 'Trave', only to be delayed further by fog. Woodhouse eventually arrived at Southampton on the 16th May 1889 and travelled to London: here he spent two nights and visited the Royal Academy before he at last headed home to Morecambe after a truly remarkable and exciting 'trip of a life time'.

After this trip Woodhouse was to produce a number of paintings depicting the many scenes, animals and buildings, which he had sketched on his travels. The following are a few of the paintings, which began to appear at various exhibitions after his return to England:

Gibraltar
Off Gibraltar
'Moss Brow' off Gibraltar
Port Said
Fruit Market, Port Said
Port Said, studies of Egyptian Mules
Camels
Egyptian Cattle Market
Entrance to the Black Sea
A Caique on the Bosphorus[1] (a light rowing-boat)
On the Bosphorus[1]
Constantinople
Seraglio Point, Constantinople
Sophia Steps, Constantinople
A shot at the Slaver (See Exhibition chapter)
Dutch Fishers
Dutch Craft on the Weser

Notes

No.1   The modern spelling is usually Bosporus

The Moss Brow.   Watercolour.
Private collection

At the end of March 1889 William Woodhouse boarded the Moss Brow at Cardiff and sailed
on her to Constantinople.

An extract from Woodhouse's diary dated Wednesday 10th April 1889.

10 Wednesday
Fresh breeze. Sketching until 2 o'clock. Since we left Gibraltar we
loose 20 minutes each day. Several swallows came aboard today
and alighted within a yard of me. Since Monday we have not seen
land and shall not see any until we arrive at Port Said on Saturday.
Distance from Cardiff to Port Said 3187 miles 1916 from Gib to
Port Said.

Rounding the Rock of Gibraltar.   Watercolour.
Private collection

Sophia Steps, Constantinople.   Watercolour.
Private collection

Maria Emsley. Watercolour.
Private collection

Painted in 1889 before her marriage to William Woodhouse. Maria is dressed in a robe,
which William probably brought back from his Near East trip.

Copy of the telegram, which William Woodhouse received on his arrival at Bremerhaven.
Courtesy of Lancaster City Museums

CHAPTER 6

WILLIAM WOODHOUSE   - Royal Academy of Arts Exhibits.

Woodhouse always shunned the limelight and was not interested in pushing himself into the public eye or courting publicity, so it was probably with some reluctance that he was persuaded to submit any pictures to the Royal Academy of Arts at all.

'Doomed'

In 1889, just before Woodhouse embarked on his tour of the Near East, he submitted his painting 'Doomed' to The Royal Academy at Burlington House, London. Not only was it accepted but it was hung 'on the line', that is in prime viewing position. This action bears witness to the selection committee's acknowledgement and approval of Woodhouse's talent. Woodhouse was to hear of this grand success when the ship he was travelling on docked at Bremerhaven on his return journey.

'Doomed' is an oil painting of a Buffalo standing on a slight mound, which is covered in snow, surrounded by a pack of attacking wolves.   With its head down Woodhouse captured the defiant expression in the buffalo's eye perfectly, and we are left in no doubt that the animal is not going to be killed without first putting up a valiant fight.

The painting was sold on the first day of the exhibition and bought by The Right Honourable Alexander Staveley-Hill, MP, QC, a famous big game hunter and one of the greatest authorities on Canada in Parliament.   He was Managing Director of Oxley Ranching in Canada, which was founded in 1882. Staveley Hill in Alberta, Canada is named after him. The consideration for this painting was £40.

'Wolves and Wild Boar'

Woodhouse did not submit another painting to the Royal Academy until 1896, this was entitled 'Wolves and Wild Boar', and once again it was snapped up immediately.   The painting depicts two very savage wolves with cruel glints in their eyes and vicious expressions. They have just brought down a boar, which appears to have given up its fight for survival. Even the snowy plain seems to emit a cold menacing feeling.   The Duchess of Bedford[1] bought it for the consideration of £30. She was obviously impressed with his work and Woodhouse sent her photographs of other 'Big Game Subjects' he had painted. Her Grace asked to view the original paintings but by then only two remained unsold and were hanging at exhibitions elsewhere in the country. The painting of Wolves and Wild Boar remains in His Grace the Duke of Bedford's Art Collection; it is the only Woodhouse painting he possesses.

Before the end of the exhibition the Honorary Secretary of the Council of the Royal Birmingham Society of Artists wrote to Woodhouse to 'specially invite' him to contribute his picture of 'Wolves and Wild Boar' for hanging at their Autumn Exhibition. Both he and his society colleagues had seen it and viewed it with pleasure. However as it had already been sold this was of course, not possible. It was to be another fifteen years before Woodhouse submitted a picture to the Royal Academy.

Doomed. Oil.
Courtesy of Lancaster City Museums

Royal Academy of Arts,

LONDON, W.,

May 10 1889

Sir

I HAVE to inform you that your work No. *1089*

in the Catalogue of the ROYAL ACADEMY for the present year, entitled

'Doomed'

and priced £ *40* , has been selected for purchase by

A. Stavely Hill Esq MP

4 Queens Gate

As the ROYAL ACADEMY only undertakes to register the selection of works, it is left to the Artist to communicate with the Purchaser in reference to the payment and delivery of the work at the close of the Exhibition.

I am, *Sir*

Your obedient Servant,

Registrar

W. Woodhouse Esq

Copy of the letter sent to William Woodhouse by the Royal Academy of Arts informing him of the sale of his exhibit "Doomed" to The Right Honourable Alexander Stavely-Hill MP, QC.

Courtesy of Lancaster City Museums

·ROYAL·ACADEMY·OF·ARTS·

The President and Council

request the honour of the company of

Mr W Woodhouse

on Wednesday, June 26th at nine o'clock.

Evening Dress.

Fred. A. Eaton

Secretary.

Single Admission.   *This Card to be produced.*   *Not transferable.*

An invitation from the Royal Academy of Arts 1889
Courtesy of Lancaster City Museums

NOT TRANSFERABLE.

ROYAL ACADEMY OF ARTS,

1896.

Mr W. Woodhouse

*is invited to inspect such of his Works as have been accepted
for Exhibition on Monday, April 27th.*

FRED. A. EATON, *Sec.*

N.B.—This ticket is issued as a personal admission, and can only be used by the
Exhibitor named on it.

The Galleries will be open from 9 a.m. till 7 p.m.

Admission Ticket, Royal Academy of Arts 1896
Courtesy of Lancaster City Museums

Wolves and Wild Boar.   Oil.
Royal Academy of Arts Exhibit 1896

By kind permission of His Grace the Duke of Bedford and the Trustees of the Bedford Estates

Royal Academy of Arts,

LONDON, W.

April, 1911.

SIR, OR MADAM,

Your oil picture, as per the enclosed label, being not more than six feet sight measurement in the largest dimension, having been placed on the line, may have glass put over it, if so desired.

Should you wish to avail yourself of this privilege, the glass—*with the enclosed gummed label attached to it*—must be delivered at the **Burlington Gardens entrance, not later than 6 p.m. on Monday, April 24.**

I am,

Your obedient Servant,

FRED. A. EATON,
Secretary.

Copy of the letter sent to Woodhouse by the Royal Academy of Arts,
which refers to his painting "Vanquished" 1911
Courtesy of Lancaster City Museums

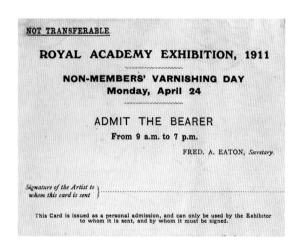

NOT TRANSFERABLE.

ROYAL ACADEMY EXHIBITION, 1911

NON-MEMBERS' VARNISHING DAY
Monday, April 24

ADMIT THE BEARER
From 9 a.m. to 7 p.m.

FRED. A. EATON, *Secretary.*

Signature of the Artist to whom this card is sent } . . . .

This Card is issued as a personal admission, and can only be used by the Exhibitor
to whom it is sent, and by whom it must be signed.

Admission Ticket, Royal Academy of Arts 1911
Courtesy of Lancaster City Museums

'Vanquished'

The third and final painting to be exhibited and 'hung on the line' was 'Vanquished' in 1911. This painting again in oils, depicts two moose or elk bulls at the edge of a Canadian lake in the twilight. Across the lake in the distance can be seen hills and a pine forest. The 'vanquished' lies exhausted on the ground whilst the victor stands proudly and triumphantly over him.

Once again Woodhouse managed to portray the power and might of these beasts with his anatomical understanding and technical abilities. This time the work was not sold at the exhibition and although it appeared at other exhibitions it remained unsold. It was kept in the Woodhouse family collection until after Winnie's death when it was bequeathed to the Lancaster City Museum Art Collection.

Vanquished. Oil.
Courtesy of Lancaster City Museums

Royal Academy of Arts Exhibit for 1911
Unfortunately this painting was in its present poor condition when it was bequeathed to the Lancaster City Museum.

The Royal Academy of Arts is the oldest fine arts institution in Britain. It was founded in London in 1768 under the patronage of George III. The early art exhibitions were held at Pall Mall, Somerset House and the National Gallery, London. In 1869 the Academy moved to Burlington House, Piccadilly, and it was to this address that William submitted his three paintings for the Committee's consideration and acceptance. A prestigious event on any artist's calendar, the exhibition ran from the first Monday in May until the following August Bank Holiday.

Notes

No.1   Mary, Duchess of Bedford was the wife of Herbrand-Arthur Russell, 11th Duke of Bedford and known as the 'Flying Duchess'. In the late 1920's her daring flights were far more adventurous than today's travels. Basically she was an unconventional Duchess, who shunned the High Life. She had a great love of animals and collected many paintings, so it was not surprising when she purchased Woodhouse's painting of Wolves and Wild Boar for her collection.

William Woodhouse in his studio – Auburn Court.
Courtesy of Lancaster City Museums

CHAPTER 7

WILLIAM WOODHOUSE – Exhibitions 1881 to date.

To find dates, locations and catalogue listings of the following exhibitions, please turn to the appendices at the back of this book.

William Woodhouse's work has been exhibited at Galleries around the British Isles since about 1881. The majority of the exhibitions appear to have been held in the North West of England, where Woodhouse was always a popular artist. Some exhibitions were large and included many of his paintings while others were on a much smaller scale and only one or two of his pictures were on view.

In general the exhibitions from 1881 to 1926 only displayed a few of Woodhouse's paintings as he strove to make a name for himself in the art world. His endeavours to get his work known started in earnest in 1881, when he had two oil paintings exhibited at the Mechanics Institute, Lancaster. Gradually during the 1880's and 1890's more of his work was to be seen, including an oil painting hung at the Royal Scottish Academy in 1883. With the 1900's came a change in artistic preferences, and Woodhouse started to produce more watercolour paintings of local scenes and industries. Some of these appeared at an exhibition held at Lancaster in 1908. Two paintings were accepted by the Royal Institute of Painters in Watercolours in 1911, with a further watercolour exhibited by the Institute in 1925. (Appendix II)

In 1925 the artist Sydney Paviere was appointed the Art Director and Curator of the Harris Museum and Art Gallery at Preston, Lancashire. Keen to promote the work of local artists, Paviere held an exhibition in 1926, which was open to Lancashire born artists living within the county. It was a very popular event with both the artists and the general public. It gave the visitors an opportunity to purchase paintings at affordable prices with the prospect of their pictures increasing in value if the artist became well known.

As the exhibition was so successful it became an annual event. These Spring Exhibitions gave Woodhouse the opportunity to have his work accepted by the committee and displayed every year until his death. It was therefore fitting that after Woodhouse's death in January 1939, Paviere, who had become a close friend, arranged a memorial exhibition of Woodhouse's work. It was held in conjunction with the 1939 Spring Exhibition. Some of Woodhouse's paintings were on loan from family and friends while others were for sale. Prices ranged from 2 guineas to 12 guineas (now £2.10 to £12.60). One must bear in mind inflation rates: at the time an A.R.P. Warden might have earned £3 a week, while an Agricultural Labourer's wage was under £2 a week. Also on view for the first time was the last picture painted by Woodhouse, it was entitled 'The Blacksmith'. This painting was completed the day before he died.

This was not the last time that Woodhouse's work was seen at the Harris exhibitions, as paintings appeared in 1940, 1943 and 1944. The last catalogue reference for Woodhouse appears to be in 1949, ten years after his death and twenty-two years after his first paintings were accepted, a great achievement for any artist. It was a tribute to Sydney Paviere too, as twenty years after he first conceived the idea to hold these exhibitions they were still drawing the crowds, with thirty thousand visitors looking at five hundred paintings.
(Appendix III)

Regionally, Woodhouse was very fortunate to have had a 'champion' in Paviere, whose belief in him as an accomplished artist was well justified. An exhibition of Woodhouse's work at the Harris Gallery in 1927 attracted over ten thousand people. The majority of the paintings were of animals and birds, with a few pictures from around the Skipton area in Yorkshire. Twenty-three paintings were sold during the exhibition, although it was not only the general public who were busy buying pictures. Preston Corporation bought three watercolours for their permanent Art Collection. At this exhibition Sydney Paviere first used the much quoted phrase, *"Good pictures are like good wine, need no praise; let them speak for themselves".* What praise indeed for William Woodhouse and his paintings.
(Appendix IV)

Snow Leopard. Watercolour.
Courtesy of Harris Museum and Art Gallery, Preston, Lancashire

A Shot at the Slaver.   Watercolour.
Courtesy of Harris Museum and Art Gallery, Preston, Lancashire

'Snow Leopard', 'A Shot at the Slaver' and 'Shrimpers' were three watercolours purchased after the "Loan Exhibition of Paintings" held at the Harris Museum and Art Gallery in December 1927

Shrimpers.   Watercolour.
Courtesy of Harris Museum and Art Gallery, Preston, Lancashire

Snipe.   Watercolour.
Courtesy of Harris Museum and Art Gallery, Preston, Lancashire

This watercolour was purchased after the 'Fifth Annual Spring Exhibition of Pictures by
Lancashire Artists' held at the Harris Museum and Art Gallery in April/May 1930

In 1931 another friend of Woodhouse's, Gilbert Bland, the Borough Librarian and Curator of the museum in Lancaster, arranged one of the biggest and most ambitious exhibition. It showed oils and watercolours by Woodhouse along with etchings and dry points by his son Roy. In April a letter was sent out to local collectors requesting the loan of 'William Woodhouse' works. Thirty-four people lent paintings, including eight family members. Out of the total two hundred and fifty-six pictures exhibited, one hundred and ninety works were by William Woodhouse. Judging by the many glowing newspaper reports of the time the critics loved him, commenting on the high quality of his work and his ability to express himself on canvas.

A sample of the quotes extracted from local Morecambe and Lancaster newspapers:

"The paintings are bright and life-like especially those of game birds and dogs. The various attitudes of his subjects and the beautiful plumage allow William to infuse true colours, which immediately catch one's attention".

"It is surprising that work of such high quality is not better known, not only locally but to a much wider circle of art lovers".

"One finds frequent and amusing indications that his love lies with the 'lower' animals, sometimes the landscape vies with the animals but in most cases the honours are with the animals and birds".

"A naturalist by heart, who has the twofold gift of understanding and loving nature, and being able to express his thoughts on canvas."

"One of the chief features that commend the exhibition to local visitors is the numbers of local scenes".

Educational visits to the exhibition were encouraged, and both teachers and school children had found them enjoyable and instructive. Two radio broadcasts about 'Art in the North of England' mentioned the exhibition and William Woodhouse on their programmes. This may be commonplace today but, in the 1930's, was considered quite an event!
Appendix V)

A large exhibition of William and Roy's work was held at the former Council Offices at Heysham[1] in 1933. During the ceremony Councillor A.W. Gorton stated that he and William Woodhouse had been school friends, and that when they were both young men attitudes had been morally, socially, physically and religiously far better than the current post war days, and that Woodhouse's paintings reflected these old Victorian and Edwardian periods when life was quite different. Once again the exhibition was a great success with the critics praising a number of Woodhouses's works. It was quoted that *"William Woodhouse was one of Morecambe's sons, a great painter but too modest"!*
(Appendix VI)

Borough of Lancaster. Public Library, Museum, and Art Gallery.

TELEPHONE: LANCASTER 730.

G. M. BLAND, F.R.G.S., M.R.S.L.,
BOROUGH LIBRARIAN AND CURATOR.

Public Library,
Storey Institute,

Lancaster, 21st April 1931.

Dear

Woodhouse Exhibition.

It is proposed to hold an Exhibition of works by William Woodhouse, in the Lancaster Art Gallery, Storey Institute, for six weeks commencing 9th June next.

My Storey Institute & Library Committee desire your practical interest in this Exhibition, and will be very grateful if you will loan the example/s of the Artist's work named below - X. It is intended to make this Exhibition thoroughly representative of the work of this well-known local Artist. Admission to the Gallery will be free, and a catalogue published.

Any pictures you may care to loan will be collected, and covered by insurance until their safe return to you after the Exhibition.

If you are willing to lend the exhibit/s requested will you kindly notify me not later than Monday, 4th May next, when I will send you particulars regarding Collection, etc.

Yours truly,

[signature]

Borough Librarian & Curator.

X.

P.S. It will greatly facilitate the work of the Curator if you will kindly affix your name and address to any work loaned by you.

Letter requesting "Loan of Paintings" for the Exhibition of Woodhouse paintings in 1931
Courtesy of Lancaster City Museums

Invitation to the "Private View" of Oils, Watercolours and Etchings
by William and Roy Woodhouse.
Courtesy of Lancaster City Museums

Photograph of 'the Notabilities' at the opening of the Lancaster Exhibition in 1931
Courtesy of Lancaster Reference Library

When Woodhouse was well into his late seventies, six bird paintings were exhibited at both Oxford and Bristol in 1934.
(Appendix VII)

With the Second World War following shortly after his death, Woodhouse seemed to fade into the shadows as the Country prepared for war. It was not until the 1970's and 1980's when large exhibitions of his paintings were once again mounted, that there was a sustained revival of interest in his work. Previously unseen paintings were shown alongside his original much-admired pictures, as ardent art lovers sought his work. In 1974 Woodhouse's paintings were displayed at an exhibition held at the Lancaster City Museum. All the paintings belonged to the museum's own art collection and featured two other local artists, Reginald Aspinwall and Robert Rampling who had been painting at the end of the nineteenth century and the beginning of the twentieth. While William Woodhouse was by far the least well represented artist with only four oil and six watercolour paintings on show, he was probably the most versatile and accomplished artist of the three.
Appendix VIII)

One of the largest and most inspiring exhibitions of Woodhouse's work staged outside Lancashire came about quite by accident. In 1975 Roy placed half a dozen of his father's paintings in a Sussex auction hoping to raise some interest in his work. David McDonald Booth, a gallery owner, was at the auction. He liked Woodhouse's work and bought some of his paintings. Some time later a chance meeting at Bisley between Roy and Mrs. Bruno Schroder, a well-known rifle shot and friend of the McDonald Booths, led to Roy getting in touch with David. Amazed at the amount of Woodhouse's work still in the family's possession, David decided to hold an exhibition at his Kensington Gallery in London, designed to portray how Woodhouse had created his paintings, from the early sketches to the completed works. It must have been exciting for Roy and Winnie to see their father's drawings, watercolours and oil paintings once again catching the public's eye.
(Appendix IX)

With the renewed interest in Woodhouse's work gathering momentum and art collectors, together with the general public, wanting to see and own more of his paintings, the Cumbrian Fine Arts Gallery in Kirkby Lonsdale held an exhibition of Woodhouse's work at its gallery in 1977. From opening night until the exhibition closed the gallery was inundated with visitors. Once again Roy and Winnie loaned several pieces of work. Alongside old favourites were items not previously exhibited, including a Linthorpe vase[2], which was hand painted by Woodhouse portraying an avocet, and a terracotta sculpture of a bison. The log of his voyage to the Far East and the telegram he received advising him of his first Royal Academy acceptance were exhibited.
(Appendix X)

The Lower Nupend Gallery near Malvern in Worcestershire hosted 'The Glimmering Landscape Show' in 1980 and on view were a pair of Woodhouse watercolours. One was dated 1884 and featured the Old Harbour in Morecambe, a sight very familiar to Woodhouse when he lived at Queens Terrace overlooking the sea. One of Woodhouse's classic oil paintings of 'Donkeys on the Beach' was presented for sale at the gallery's Christmas exhibition, which took place to raise money for the Red Cross.

In 1981 the Lancaster City Museum held an exhibition entitled 'A Century's Span' which displayed both William and Roy Woodhouse's work. So keen were family, friends and collectors to lend paintings for this exhibition that, together with paintings from the museum's own art collection, it became over subscribed and the Museum ran out of hanging space. Woodhouse's earliest known dated work, a portrait of Robert Baxter in a top hat with his horse and dog painted in 1877, was on view along with fifty-eight other paintings. With Roy still happily painting in 1981 it meant that father and son together had 'notched' up over a hundred years as artists – A Century's Span. To mark the occasion Roy and Winnie presented to the museum a portrait of their mother, Maria Elizabeth, painted by their father. (Appendix XI)

Oils, watercolours and pencil drawings adorned the walls of Lancaster City Museum when an exhibition, "A Great Love of Nature, the Artistry of William Woodhouse" was held in 1989 to commemorate the fiftieth anniversary of Woodhouse's death. A conscious decision was made to include as much Woodhouse work as possible into the exhibition from private collections. This was designed to get rarely seen paintings into the public domain. Owners of Woodhouse's work did not let the museum down, and a diverse selection of pictures was displayed with other memorabilia to show that Woodhouse's interests had spread far and wide. Some works touched on the exotic while others showed animals in their wild environments. After three months more than ten thousand visitors had visited the exhibition, showing that Woodhouse's work still held its appeal. This must have been very encouraging for the Museum's Curator. (Appendix XII)

During the latter part of the twentieth century, Iain Dodgson, a Lancashire art dealer who was passionate about Woodhouse's work, travelled all over the United Kingdom buying his pictures both privately and at auction. In March 1990 at Dodgson's family 'Studio Arts Gallery' in Lancaster, a unique collection of fifty-eight works by William and seventeen by Roy were offered for sale. The exhibition attracted considerable interest, as several of William's sporting pictures were included. One of the finest being oil on canvas, portraying a 'Cocker Spaniel with Game'. Another painting entitled 'Jess and Turk, Waiting for Master' was an oil painting of William's two setters which were always a great favourite with the public. 'The Sly Fox', a watercolour depicting a fox emerging from the brambles and sneaking away with a pheasant was another fine picture. (Appendix XIII)

In 1998 the Lancaster City Museum organized a temporary exhibition called 'Fine Art in Focus'. The exhibition was designed to show what went on behind the scenes at the museum: how and why they collected gifts, purchases and bequests, and how they decided what works to acquire to enhance the museum's 'Fine Art Collection'. The museum also showed how they cared for their existing collections, which included practical demonstrations by a conservator. Many of the paintings exhibited were by artists with a local connection and form part of the museum's art collection. Included was a selection of working drawings by Woodhouse together with several of his oil and watercolour pictures. One of the paintings to receive specialist attention from the conservator was a portrait by Woodhouse of his wife, Maria Elizabeth[3]. During it's cleaning it became clear that Woodhouse had changed some of the original design several times, as some areas of the portrait had been repainted. This was the first opportunity the museum had had to present most of Miss Woodhouse's bequest for public viewing.

(Appendix XIV)

Notes

No. 1   In 1928 the two separate authorities of Morecambe and Heysham amalgamated to form a local authority better able to provide services, and develop the area's tourist potential. The ceremony took place on 1st October. After speeches from a platform raised over the old district boundaries (The Battery Hotel) 2,000 ice creams were distributed to local school children. A banquet was held at Morecambe Tower Ballroom followed by dancing in the Balmoral Room.

No. 2   Linthorpe pottery was established in Middlesbrough in 1879 by John Harrison, a local entrepreneur and the designer Christopher Dresser. Although the pottery only lasted ten years it produced over 2,000 ceramic ware shapes in that time. The Dorman Museum in Middlesbrough holds a very good collection of Linthorpe pottery including the avocet vase and other pieces owned by Woodhouse and bequeathed to the museum by his daughter Winnie.

No. 3   The portrait of Maria Elizabeth can be seen in the photograph to celebrate Winnie's one hundredth birthday on page 138.

Linthorpe Vase – Hand painted by William Woodhouse.
Courtesy of Dorman Museum, Middlesbrough Council.

CHAPTER 8

WILLIAM WOODHOUSE - Book Illustrations.

William Woodhouse provided illustrations for three books:

1)   Birds of Yorkshire by Thomas H. Nelson, M.B.O.U.   (Two Volumes).

2)   Life Stories of Big Game by W.S. Chadwick.

3)   Mishi The Man-eater and Other Tales of Big Game by E.C. Stuart Baker, O.B.E
       F.Z.S., F.L.S., M.B.O.U.

1) **Birds of Yorkshire by Thomas H. Nelson.**
Published by A. Brown and Sons London, 1907.

Thomas Hudson Nelson, a friend of Woodhouse, was a well-known naturalist and
ornithologist from Redcar. He had previously lived for many years in the Bishop Auckland
area before moving to Redcar. During his lifetime he collected both birds and eggs amassing
a great collection. This was donated to the Dorman Museum, Middlesbrough in 1914. Many
of the landscape backgrounds in the bird cases were painted by Nelson and friends, which
naturally included Woodhouse. His book 'Birds of Yorkshire' is an historical account of Avi-
fauna of the county.

Two different oil paintings of Bempton Cliffs, by Woodhouse, are reproduced on the
frontispiece of each volume. A sketch for the title page was designed especially for the book.
The same picture appears in both volumes. Although Woodhouse made sketches and
drawings for both volumes, most of his work appears in the second book.

Listed below are the titles of the illustrations as they appear in the books.

Volume I
Frontispiece   A Misty Morning on the Bempton Cliffs at "Hateley Shoot".
                  Whales jaw bones near Bempton, nesting place of Blue Tit.

Volume II
Frontispiece   Cliff Climbing at Bempton, on "Old Mosey".
                  Nesting place of Cormorants near Whitby High Lights, Hawsker.
                  Grouse sitting on the roof of a moorland cottage in Teesdale, as
                  mentioned by Tunstall.
                  A Flight of Grouse.
                  MacQueens Bustard, the first of two Yorkshire examples Shot at
                  Marske-by-the-Sea.

A Teesmouth shore scene.
Large flights of Godwits and other shore-birds at the Teesmouth
in September, 1895.
Curlew perching on a post, on a moor near Harrogate.
Nesting place of Black-Headed Gull, on the moors near Whitby.
Kettleness, the nesting place of the Herring and Black-backed Gulls.
Great Northern Diver.

Grouse sitting on the roof of a moorland cottage in Teesdale, as mentioned by Tunstall.

Watercolour.

Cliff Climbing at Bempton, on "Old Mosey".   Oil.

MacQueen's Bustard

This handsome Bustard is a native of Asia, and a very rare accidental straggler to these shores. This bird was shot at Marske-by-the-Sea, Yorkshire at close range in 1892 and was badly damaged on one side. After it had been to the taxidermist's, it was eventually purchased by the Newcastle Museum. This illustration by William Woodhouse is taken from a watercolour drawing (after a photograph of the specimen).

MacQueen's Bustard.
The first of the two Yorkshire examples, shot at Marske-by-the Sea.
Watercolour.

It is interesting to note that the Bustard was probably one of the few paintings by Woodhouse of a bird that he had not shot himself.

2) **Life Stories of Big Game by W.S. Chadwick.**
Published by H.F. & G. Witherby London, 1928.

Each story is of a struggle for survival. Usually they start with the animal's birth, its fight for supremacy within the herd and its eventual death, whether against other wild animals or man. The stories set in Africa are at times savage and we are not spared the gruesome accounts of attacks or killings.

List of plates and titles:

Frontispiece   "Rolling to Earth fast locked in the Grip of a Young Male Baboon".

Facing Page   "Two Snarling Heavy Bodies were hurled Yards Distant, each with Several Broken Ribs". (Buffalo, heads down tossing the Lions aside).

"Game had been Scarce, and One Night they came across a Bush Kraal Filled with Young Cattle". (A Lion circling the camp ready to attack)

"Charge after Charge they made, first One then the Other going down Under the Shock of the Impact". (Rhinoceroses fighting).

"A Band of Yelling Natives jeered delightedly at the Huddled Body of the twenty-foot Crocodile".

"In the Centre of the Circle a great Shaggy Lion feasted busily".

The posture of these animals in Woodhouse's sketches captures the sense of 'the law of the jungle', and the fight for survival, they add the required menacing touch to the author's stories.

"Rolling to Earth fast locked in the Grip of a Young Male Baboon".
Watercolour.

"Charge after Charge they made, first One then the other going down under the Shock of the Impact".   Watercolour.

"A Band of Yelling Natives jeered delightedly at the Huddled Body of the Twenty – foot Crocodile".   Watercolour.

3) Mishi The Man-Eater and Other Tales of Big Game by E.C. Stuart Baker.
Published by H.F. & G. Witherby London, Circa 1930.

The author, Stuart Baker, spent fifteen years in one of the wildest parts of India and his work involved close contact with the various tribesmen who lived in this region. He was devoted to Big Game Shooting, hunting Tigers, Leopards, Bears, Buffalo, Deer and occasionally Rhinoceroses.

The first story begins with a famous man-eating tiger. Initially written as though the story-teller is the tiger, giving an account of his early life and career spent as 'a mean and ferocious' man-eater, the author then takes over, and with continued zeal, tells us how he ended the monster's reign of terror! The other chapters are adventure stories experienced by Stuart Baker involving animals of the Big Game Kingdom.

List of plates and titles:

Frontispiece	"Here I dropped the body to the ground by the edge of the water". (Shows a Tiger with the body of a tribesman).
Facing Page	"I had just started my evening prowl when I came to a rice-field". (Tiger). "Charged and caught one of the villagers with her right horn". (A fierce looking buffalo stands snorting over an injured tribeswoman). "His whole attitude breathed such indignation and defiance that he made a grand sight". (Buffalo).

Woodhouse's drawings show the power of these animals and their utter disregard for man.

Copies of Woodhouse's paintings have appeared occasionally on the front cover of various magazines.

In 1893, the magazine "Black and White", a weekly illustrated review which incorporated "The Pictorial World", featured a woodcut illustration of one of Woodhouse's paintings of a puppy entitled "Is This Life Worth Living". At the time Woodhouse's painting was on show at the Newcastle Art Gallery.

Perhaps a rather dog-eared copy of the publication! This is hardly surprising as the photograph shows an original copy of the 1893 front cover, which belonged to Woodhouse.

Private collection

The Christmas edition of The Field magazine, dated 17th November 1966 featured a copy of Woodhouse's painting entitled 'Duck Shooting' on its front cover. A copy of this painting can be seen framed, on the wall behind Winnie, in the photograph taken to celebrate her one hundredth birthday on page 138.

On the inside cover of the magazine an article by F. Warner Hill posed the question of how a twentieth century spaniel could be sitting with a shooter dressed in Regency clothes. As the sportsman was wearing the right apparel and was holding a gun that was appropriate for the Regency period, Warner Hill felt that the dog was either copied from another artist's painting or could be a champion spaniel named Flint of Avendale, which could have been painted by Woodhouse during the mid 1920's. Roy refuted the idea about the spaniel, especially as his father had never copied another painter's work and as far as he was aware had not painted Flint either. He felt it was more likely that the dog had belonged to one of Woodhouse's shooting friends, and that the rest was down to 'artistic license'.

The cover of the Shooting Times and Country Magazine 29th July to 4th August 1976 featured one of Woodhouse's sporting pictures. It showed 'three gundogs with game at the end of the day'. Winnie also had a framed copy of this picture on a wall at Auburn Court.

Resting. Oil.
Courtesy of Lancaster City Museums

CHAPTER 9

WILLIAM WOODHOUSE - Comparisons and Contemporaries.

When Woodhouse started out to make a name for himself as an artist, one of the great masters of animal paintings, Sir Edwin Landseer's career had drawn to an end, although the Landseer School of painting was still popular.

Sir Edwin Landseer (1802-1873)

Sir Edwin Landseer began sketching animals from an early age and like **George Stubbs** (1724-1806), a Lancashire artist, believed in a practical knowledge of an animal's anatomy. Landseer was only twelve years old when he exhibited at the Royal Academy for the first time. After this success he had quickly established a reputation for himself and eventually became one of Queen Victoria's favourite artists. Two of Landseer's famous paintings, 'The Monarch of the Glen' and 'Stag at Bay', were painted on location in Scotland and are meticulously accurate in every detail. Landseer was without doubt one of the best animal painters of his time. He was highly respected in aristocratic society and at the Royal Academy, where a total of 179 of his pictures were exhibited.

Richard Andsell (1815-1885)

Another great Lancashire artist was Richard Andsell. When his popularity was increasing Andsell moved to London to work for a time, establishing himself as an artist of merit. Andsell too loved the Highlands of Scotland and painted Landseer-type works; stags in glens, moorland scenes, cattle and shooting parties. He also painted historical and battle scenes.

Many of Woodhouse's admirers speculated on whether he would follow in Andsell's footsteps and eventually take over the mantle left by the master. To achieve this though, Woodhouse needed to have been far better known outside Lancashire and the North of England. He would almost certainly have had to move to a studio in London, courted public attention and surrounded himself with patrons. However Woodhouse was not prepared to do this, steadfastly staying in Morecambe surrounded by all that was dear to him. He had a spirit of adventure, as his Near East trip shows, so he would not have been daunted by the prospect of moving to London. Within the family Woodhouse was known for being a quiet, retiring, modest gentleman, so perhaps the bright lights were simply not for him, and he was happy to remain in his native Lancashire away from outside pressures.

Reginald Aspinwall and Robert Rampling - contemporaries of William Woodhouse.

Reginald Aspinwall (1858-1921)

Reginald Aspinwall was born 3rd January 1858 at Preston, Lancashire. He moved to Lancaster where he too attended art classes at the Mechanics Institute, along-side

Woodhouse. Herbert Gilbert, their art master, had great hopes for Aspinwall and his artistic abilities. He was an artist with an immense talent whose work was exhibited at the Royal Academy between 1884 and 1908. Unfortunately the quality of his work varied enormously, and he was referred to as an erratic genius. Aspinwall painted many scenes around the locality, using light to create atmospheric effect. His wonderful skies with magnificent cloud formations, with the rays of the sun shining down, contrived to give his work a romantic and tranquil feeling. Sadly, towards the end of his life he was taken to the County lunatic asylum at Lancaster, where he died in impoverished circumstances.

In his obituary the following note sums up the sad position of Aspinwall:-

> *"It was the old story of 'Wine in, Wisdom out' and the nation was robbed of talent which many would have given thousands to possess".*

Robert Edward Rampling (1835-1909)
Robert Rampling was born in Liverpool and moved to Lancaster. He was mainly self-taught but caught the eye of Industrialist Edmund Sharpe who, seeing his potential, sent him to London to develop his artistic skills. It is thought that Rampling may have exhibited at the Royal Academy but no records can be found to substantiate this. Mainly a watercolourist, he painted rural scenes and evidently visited many of the sites frequented by William, especially around the Heysham area. He also painted views of Lancaster's skyline and buildings. His work was very popular; Price and Son of Lancaster reproduced some of his paintings as postcards. Rampling too sadly died in reduced circumstances in a house in Skerton, which he shared with his wife and children.

Reginald Aspinwall and Robert Rampling were probably better known than Woodhouse during their life times, although today all three artists' work is collectable.

One art critic also likened the work of Woodhouse to that of **Archibald Thorburn** and **Joseph Wolf,** feeling that he was their equal.

Archibald Thorburn (1860-1935)
Archibald Thorburn was described as an animal painter and illustrator. His main topics were animals, birds and flowers. He was born in Scotland, and from an early age loved all aspects of nature. He was taught to draw and paint by his father who was the miniaturist to Queen Victoria. Most of his works were set in the South East of England, the countryside where he lived or in the Highlands of Scotland, which he loved. Thorburn specialized in studies of game birds, concentrating on their plumage and habitat. He was perhaps best known as a book illustrator of birds, his first work being published in 1883. Woodhouse and Thorburn certainly appear to have painted very similar pictures, with both artists preferring to go out into the field to sketch from life and being meticulous in their eye for detail.

Joseph Wolf (1820-1899)

Joseph Wolf was also an illustrator and painter of animals and birds. Born in Germany he too spent many hours watching and sketching birds. He went first to Antwerp in Belguim and studied drawing techniques, then to London in 1848 where he worked at the British Museum. He illustrated a number of natural history books and made drawings for the Zoological Society. Two of his most important works were drawings for John Gould's "Birds of Great Britain" and "Birds of Asia".

Both of these artists exhibited at the Royal Academy and at other exhibitions around the country.

Roses from the garden of a house named Zetland Ville.   Oil.
Zetland Ville was once the home of friends of the Woodhouse family.
Courtesy of Lancaster City Museums

CHAPTER 10

WILLIAM WOODHOUSE - Family History.

William's Parents - James and Hannah Woodhouse (nee Baxter).

James Woodhouse was born 11[1] October 1819 the son of William and Betty Woodhouse of Poulton[1], Lancashire. He was the ninth child out of a family of eleven children. They were all baptized at the Chapelry of Poulton and lived at Poulton Square, which was the centre of the village. William was a yeoman farmer who owned land commonly known as Mill Stoop according to a survey of 1824.

Hannah Baxter was born 19th April 1823 the daughter of Thomas and Mary Baxter. She was the fourth of eight children, six of whom were boys. Hannah was also baptized at the Chapelry, and lived in Poulton village where her father was a farmer too.

At this time Poulton had no promenade, just the sea and shore. Water was drawn from a well in the square and there was an open sewer. Fish refuse and garbage rotted in the street, making manure for the land!   It was dirty, smelt dreadful and diseases such as cholera flourished.

On the1851 census James aged 31 years was a fisherman who lived at home with his widowed father, two of his brothers and a sister. Hannah also lived at home with her parents and brothers. Her father Thomas owned a sixty-acre farm and employed four men, becoming a director on the first local Board of Health for Poulton, Bare and Torrisholme in 1852.

On 27th March 1853 James and Hannah were married at St. Mary's Parish Church, Lancaster. They began married life living in a fisherman's cottage in Morecambe Street: it would have been a hard life by today's standard. Here four of their children were born and baptized at the Holy Trinity Church, Poulton:

Mary	1854 - 1933
Elizabeth	1855 - 1924
William	**1857 - 1939**
Emily	1859 - 1946

On 14[th]June 1860 Hannah's father Thomas died, followed on 6th January 1861 by James's father William, both men left land and property. James and Hannah's circumstances improved, and with their children they moved to Queens Terrace, into a fairly new house over looking the seashore. It was here that their fifth and last child was born:

Alfred	1862 – 1943

Queens Terrace, the houses on the left hand side of the photograph. The new pier in the
foreground was built circa 1868-69.
James and Hannah moved to Queens Terrace around 1861.
Courtesy of Lancashire County Library North Division Morecambe Library & Information Service

Poulton le Sands began to flourish and expand. James and Hannah invested in land and
property including 'lodging houses', although for a few years James continued his work as a
fisherman. However, by 1871, the rents from lodging houses and repayments from money
lent for mortgages provided them with their income and they appeared to prosper. When
James died from typhoid on 5th June1874, aged 54 years he was described as a yeoman farmer
and boatman, having been Secretary of the Steamboat Company.

Hannah continued to live at Queens Terrace after James's death but had moved to 42 Green
Street by 1890. Both the 1881 and 1891 census show her as Head of the Household living off
her own means, and she still owned lodging houses. By 1901 she had retired and lived at 1
Edward Street with her unmarried daughter Elizabeth. The rest of her children were married
and she had eleven surviving grandchildren.

Hannah died on 29th July 1916 at 9 Fairfield Road Heysham, aged 93 years. My great uncle Dr. Fred Hogarth was in attendance.

Both James and Hannah Woodhouse are buried in Holy Trinity Churchyard Morecambe, as are their parents.

Notes

No. 1   Poulton was one of three villages that would later be known as Morecambe. The other two are Bare and Torrisholme.

William Woodhouse (right) with George Holden.   Photograph.
Courtesy of Lancaster City Museums

George Holden was a great friend of William Woodhouse's and the two of them spent many happy hours in Woodhouse's studio. George found William extremely kind and a good sport: they always enjoyed going on shooting expeditions together.

THE WOODHOUSE FAMILY

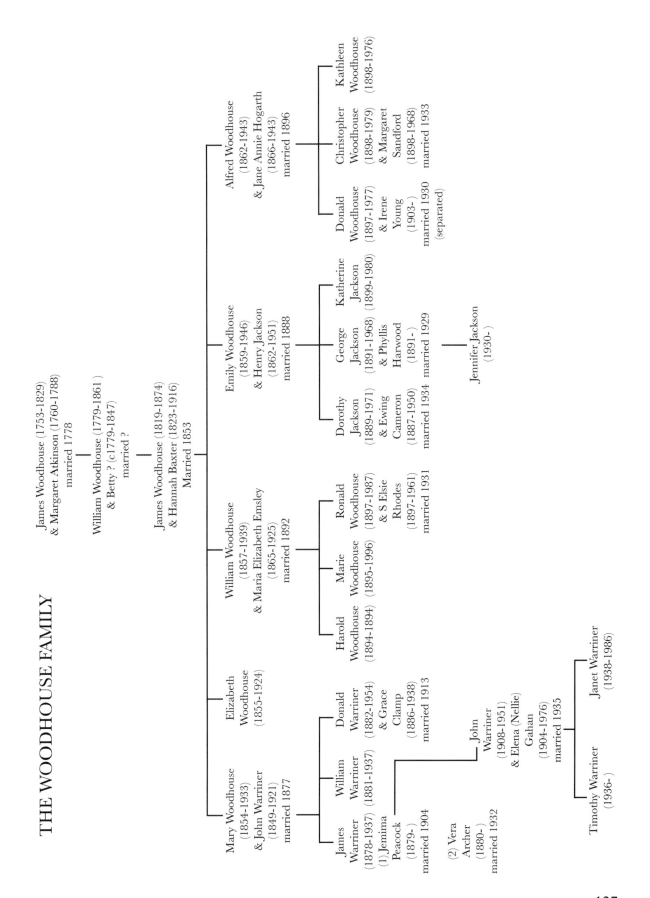

James Woodhouse (1753-1829)
& Margaret Atkinson (1760-1788)
married 1778

William Woodhouse (1779-1861)
& Betty ? (c1779-1847)
married ?

James Woodhouse (1819-1874)
& Hannah Baxter (1823-1916)
Married 1853

Mary Woodhouse
(1854-1933)
& John Warriner
(1849-1921)
married 1877

Elizabeth
Woodhouse
(1855-1924)

William Woodhouse
(1857-1939)
& Maria Elizabeth Emsley
(1865-1925)
married 1892

Emily Woodhouse
(1859-1946)
& Henry Jackson
(1862-1951)
married 1888

Alfred Woodhouse
(1862-1943)
& Jane Annie Hogarth
(1866-1943)
married 1896

James Warriner
(1878-1937)
(1) Jemima
Peacock
(1879-)
married 1904

(2) Vera
Archer
(1880-)
married 1932

William
Warriner
(1881-1937)

Donald
Warriner
(1882-1954)
& Grace
Clamp
(1886-1938)
married 1913

John
Warriner
(1908-1951)
& Elena (Nellie)
Gahan
(1904-1976)
married 1935

Timothy Warriner
(1936-)

Janet Warriner
(1938-1986)

Harold
Woodhouse
(1894-1894)

Marie
Woodhouse
(1895-1996)

Ronald
Woodhouse
(1897-1987)
& S Elsie
Rhodes
(1897-1961)
married 1931

Dorothy
Jackson
(1889-1971)
& Ewing
Cameron
(1887-1950)
married 1934

George
Jackson
(1891-1968)
& Phyllis
Harwood
(1891-)
married 1929

Katherine
Jackson
(1899-1980)

Jennifer Jackson
(1930-)

Donald
Woodhouse
(1897-1977)
& Irene
Young
(1903-)
married 1930
(separated)

Christopher
Woodhouse
(1898-1979)
& Margaret
Sandford
(1898-1968)
married 1933

Kathleen
Woodhouse
(1898-1976)

127

The Family of William Woodhouse 1896
Courtesy of Lancaster City Museums

BACK ROW - left to right - (Standing).

| Donald Warriner | James Warriner | Alfred Woodhouse | Elizabeth Woodhouse (seated) | Jane Woodhouse | Emily Jackson (seated) | Henry Jackson | William Warriner | Mary Warriner |

FRONT ROW – left to right – (Sitting).

| William Woodhouse (kneeling) | Maria Woodhouse | Marie * Woodhouse (on mother's lap) | Dorothy Jackson | Hannah Woodhouse | George Jackson (child) | John Warriner |

*known as Winnie

THE BAXTER FAMILY

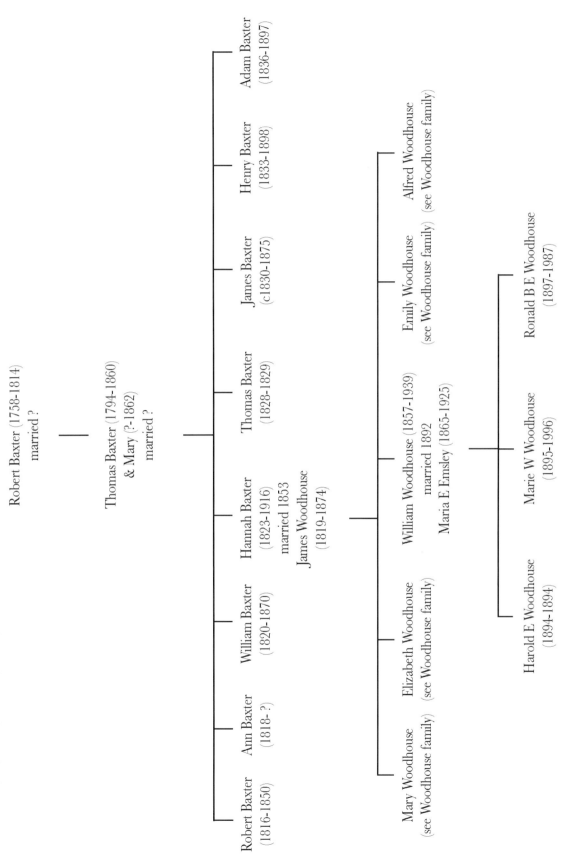

Robert Baxter (1758-1814)
married ?

Thomas Baxter (1794-1860)
& Mary (?-1862)
married ?

Robert Baxter
(1816-1850)

Ann Baxter
(1818- ?)

William Baxter
(1820-1870)

Hannah Baxter
(1823-1916)
married 1853
James Woodhouse
(1819-1874)

Thomas Baxter
(1828-1829)

James Baxter
(c1830-1875)

Henry Baxter
(1833-1898)

Adam Baxter
(1836-1897)

Mary Woodhouse
(see Woodhouse family)

Elizabeth Woodhouse
(see Woodhouse family)

William Woodhouse (1857-1939)
married 1892
Maria E Emsley (1865-1925)

Emily Woodhouse
(see Woodhouse family)

Alfred Woodhouse
(see Woodhouse family)

Harold E Woodhouse
(1894-1894)

Marie W Woodhouse
(1895-1996)

Ronald B E Woodhouse
(1897-1987)

THE EMSLEY FAMILY

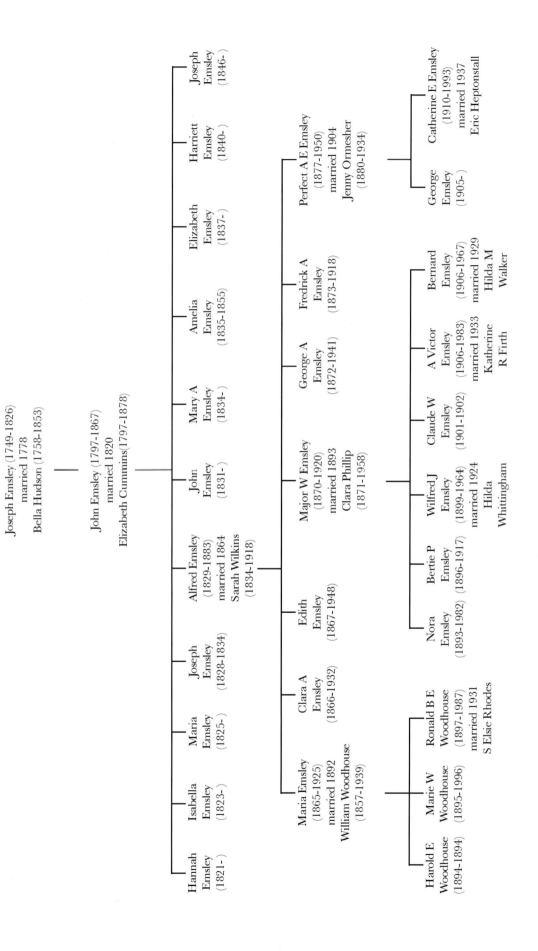

Joseph Emsley (1749-1826)
married 1778
Bella Hudson (1758-1853)

John Emsley (1797-1867)
married 1820
Elizabeth Cummins(1797-1878)

Hannah Emsley (1821-)

Isabella Emsley (1823-)

Maria Emsley (1825-)

Joseph Emsley (1828-1834)

Alfred Emsley (1829-1883) married 1864 Sarah Wilkins (1834-1918)

John Emsley (1831-)

Mary A Emsley (1834-)

Amelia Emsley (1835-1855)

Elizabeth Emsley (1837-)

Harriett Emsley (1840-)

Joseph Emsley (1846-)

Maria Emsley (1865-1925) married 1892 William Woodhouse (1857-1939)

Clara A Emsley (1866-1932)

Edith Emsley (1867-1948)

Major W Emsley (1870-1920) married 1893 Clara Phillip (1871-1958)

George A Emsley (1872-1941)

Fredrick A Emsley (1873-1918)

Perfect A E Emsley (1877-1950) married 1904 Jenny Ormesher (1880-1934)

Harold E Woodhouse (1894-1894)

Marie W Woodhouse (1895-1996)

Ronald B E Woodhouse (1897-1987) married 1931 S Elsie Rhodes

Nora Emsley (1893-1982)

Bertie P Emsley (1896-1917)

Wilfred J Emsley (1899-1964) married 1924 Hilda Whittingham

Claude W Emsley (1901-1902)

A Victor Emsley (1906-1983) married 1933 Katherine R Firth

Bernard Emsley (1906-1967) married 1929 Hilda M Walker

George Emsley (1905-)

Catherine E Emsley (1910-1993) married 1937 Eric Heptonstall

Hannah Woodhouse, nee Baxter (1823 – 1916). William's mother.
Courtesy of Lancaster City Museums

CHAPTER 11

WILLIAM WOODHOUSE - His siblings.

William had three sisters and a brother.

Mary Woodhouse

Mary was born 23rd January and baptized 26th February 1854 at Holy Trinity Church, Poulton. Mary lived with her parents, brothers and sisters until she married, working at one time as a milliner. She married John Warriner on 12th September 1877 at Holy Trinity Church, Morecambe. John, who was known as 'Jack' within the family, came from Derby where he worked as a clerk with the Midland Railway.

After their marriage, Mary and Jack lived in Derby for the rest of their lives. They had three sons:

1) James Alfred Warriner	1878 – 1937
2) William Harold Warriner	1881 – 1937
3) Donald Warriner	1882 – 1954

All three sons fought in the First World War and returned home safely.

When Jack retired from work he had been with the Midland Railway for 50 years, his last position as an outside goods manager.
Jack died 17th November 1921 and Mary died 14th November 1933.

Elizabeth Woodhouse

Elizabeth, known as Lizzie, was born 28th October and baptized 25th November 1855. Elizabeth never married and stayed at home, no doubt helping her mother with the family in the earlier days and later with the lodging houses. After her mother's death in 1916 Elizabeth moved to Leeds where she lived with her sister Emily and family. Elizabeth moved back to Morecambe and died shortly afterwards on 5th February 1924. She is the only member of the family to be buried at Torrisholme Cemetery.

Emily Woodhouse

Emily was William's youngest sister, born 22nd December 1859 and baptized 29th January 1860. Emily attended the National School as had her sisters and brothers. She lived at home with her mother, Hannah, until she married Henry Jackson, known as Harry on 18th April 1888 at the Wesleyan Chapel, Green Street, Morecambe. Harry was a bank clerk who attained the position of Bank Manager before he retired.

After their marriage Harry and Emily lived in Halifax where their three children were born:

Dorothy Jackson
(later Mrs Dorothy Cameron)   1889 - 1971

George Gilbert Jackson   1891 - 1968   (He too fought in the First World War)

Katherine Mary Jackson   1898 - 1980

In 1901 the family still lived at Halifax but had moved to Leeds by the early 1920's.
When William died in 1939, Emily was his only surviving sister, but at nearly eighty years old she was unable to attend his funeral service.

Emily died 13th April 1946 and Harry died 1st April 1951. When Harry died his daughter Dorothy was already a widow.

Alfred Woodhouse

Alfred was William's younger and only brother who was born 22nd March 1862. Like his sisters and William he was baptized at Holy Trinity Church. Alfred was 12 years old when his father died and still at school, but by 1881 he was a painter and decorator who lived and worked around Morecambe and Heysham all his life.

Alfred married Jane Annie Hogarth, my grandfather's sister, 15th January 1896 at the Wesleyan Chapel, Green Street. Jane was always known as Jeanie, and they had three children:

Donald Hogarth Woodhouse   1897 – 1977

Christopher Hogarth Woodhouse   1898 – 1979

Kathleen Alice Hannah Woodhouse   1898 –1976 Christopher and Kathleen were twins.

Alfred and Jeanie's children were baptized at the Wesleyan Chapel, Green Street, Morecambe, and Alfred became a Trustee of the Wesleyan Chapel at Sandylands, Morecambe. He was a 'Master Craftsman' and ran his own decorating business as well as being a plumber. At one time his business address was Morecambe Street, the same street where his parents had once lived. Alfred and Jeanie lived at Cross Copp, which was just around the corner from William and family. The two brothers often visited one another and liked to play dominoes in the evenings.

Jeanie died 15th September 1943 and Alfred died the following day. They were both interred at Hale Carr Cemetery, Heysham following a service at St. John's Church, Sandylands.

Mary Warriner (nee Woodhouse)
1854 – 1933 with one of her sons
Courtesy of Lancaster City Museums

John Warriner (known as Jack)
1849 – 1921
Courtesy of Lancaster City Museums

Henry (1862 – 1951) and Emily (1859 – 1946) Jackson (nee Woodhouse) with their niece
Kathleen Woodhouse (1898 – 1976).

Photograph.
Courtesy of Lancaster City Museums

Four Generations.

Left to Right

Mary Warriner   James Warriner   Hannah Woodhouse   James' son John

Courtesy of Lancaster City Museums

CHAPTER 12

WILLIAM WOODHOUSE – His Children.

Marie Winifred Woodhouse 1895-1996

William and Maria's daughter Marie was known as Winnie to her family and friends.

Winnie was born at Kenilcote on 13th April 1895 and was baptized at the Wesleyan Methodist Chapel, Green Street on 4th July. She was educated at Fylde College, Morecambe, where she successfully passed her educational examinations, including a first class pass for Freehand Drawing in 1910. Examinations were taken at the Town Hall in Lancaster, now the City Museum. Winnie enjoyed these trips to Lancaster as the pupils were allowed to go into town and visit a café after they had taken their exams, a real treat!

After leaving school Winnie studied Classical Design at the Technical School, although she was far more interested in music and played the piano. She was an accomplished pianist and continued to play until well into her nineties. Winnie was always elegant and fashion conscious. Perhaps a bit of a socialite in her younger days she loved to dance and was often seen practicing new dance steps. Although many of Winnie's values were that of the Victorian era she always liked to keep up to date with the social events of the day.

During the First World War Winnie worked for a few years at a bank, and during the Second World War became a civil servant when she joined the Post Office, remaining there for seventeen years until retiring in 1957.

Winnie never married, having lost her fiancée in the First World War. For most of her life she lived at Auburn Court with her parents eventually keeping house for both her father, and then for Roy when they became widowers. After her mother's death in 1925 Winnie took over the task of organizing afternoon teas. These were for people who would hopefully purchase Woodhouse paintings. Winnie was exceptionally proud of her father's achievements and was always happy to receive visitors who were interested in William and his work.

As a keen gardener Winnie loved her roses and the bay tree she had planted at the side of Auburn Court as a young girl. She also took great pride in producing lovely raspberries, which were happily given away to friends.

Winnie surrounded herself with her father's paintings and carefully saved cuttings from newspapers and magazines, along with catalogues and family photographs. She did not destroy anything associated with William and his art, so when she died on 17th April 1996, aged one hundred and one years, she left a house full of William Woodhouse memorabilia. It is thanks to staff at the Lancaster City Museum that this material has been catalogued and retained in their Woodhouse collection.

A photograph of Winnie taken to celebrate her 100th birthday on 13th April 1995
Private collection.

Ronald Basil Emsley Woodhouse 1897-1987

Ronald, who was known as Roy, was born 1st July 1897 at Kenilcote, the second son and youngest child of William and Maria.

He was educated at the Crookleigh Preparatory School for Boys, Cross Copp, Morecambe, before attending the George Fox School, originally the Friends School at Lancaster. In 1913 at the age of 16 years, Roy passed the University of Cambridge Board Examinations in seven subjects including Freehand, Model and Memory Drawing. He left school and worked for a short time at a bank in Windermere before he joined the army.

Roy served in the Royal Garrison Artillery. He enlisted in December 1915 and was posted to the Army Reserve. He went on active service in May 1916 as a gunner. In August he was appointed a Bombardier before receiving his commission in December 1917 when he became a Second Lieutenant. In April 1918 Roy was badly injured at Etaples, France, and spent some time in a hospital at Le Touquet before returning to England where he spent many months in army hospitals and at the Imperial Hotel at Blackpool, convalescing. He was left partially deaf from his injuries; in June 1919 he was demobilized, and afterwards went to Agricultural College at Cambridge with other army officers.

Roy Woodhouse.
Courtesy of Lancaster City Museums

Roy Woodhouse.
Convalescing at the Imperial Hotel
Blackpool.
Courtesy of Lancaster City Museums

Having attended the Morecambe School of Art, Roy took up art seriously after the war and specialized in etching. He very quickly gained a reputation; such was the quality of his work.

On 10th February 1931 Roy married **Sarah Elsie Rhodes** known as Elsie, at The Parish Church, Heysham. Elsie was the daughter of Fred Rhodes, a wool merchant and Annie Elizabeth Rhodes nee Parkinson. Elsie was born 17th March 1897 at Allerton, North Bierley, Bradford, Yorkshire, and was living at Sandylands, Morecambe when she married Roy. After their marriage they lived at Silverdale.

In June 1931 Roy exhibited some of his work with William at the Storey Institute. Sixty-five pieces were shown which included mainly etchings and dry points with a few watercolours. Some of his work was 'after his father's paintings'. He loved dogs and this was apparent by the number of 'dog portraiture' that he drew and etched. Included in the exhibition were:

Aberdeen Terrier
Airedale
Alsatian
Bloodhound
Bulldog
Chow
Clumber Spaniel
Cocker Spaniel
Dalmatian
Greyhound
Pomeranian
Setter

In 1933 Roy and William held another exhibition of their work at the former Council Offices in Heysham where Roy exhibited fifty-six etchings.

Two etchings by Roy were displayed in 1936 at the 'Eleventh Annual Spring Exhibition of Work by Lancashire Artists' at the Harris Museum and Art Gallery, Preston. They were 'The Five Sister's Window – York Minster' and 'God's Providence House – Chester'.

Roy spent time in Oxford, sketching and drawing around the Colleges as well as sketching local scenes near Morecambe: these included Levens Hall, Cartmel Priory, Brookhouse, Borwick Hall and Heysham Hall. Like his father, Roy received acclaim from the critics who thought that his etchings were particularly good. He had a great eye for detail and could copy work to perfection. By 1939 Roy had a studio in London and he sketched many scenes around the capital.

Roy and Elsie moved to Dorney, near Windsor and Eton. Roy worked in Eton, as unlike his father, he did not make his living solely as an artist. During the Second World War he served in the Taplow Home Guard, Upper Thames Patrol, from June 1940 to December 1944. Eventually Roy and Elsie retired to the south coast and lived near Bognor Regis until Elsie's death in March 1961. She is interred at St. James the Less Churchyard at Dorney. At this time Roy described himself as a retired cine equipment manager.

Roy returned to Auburn Court and shared the house with his sister, Winnie. Being a heavy smoker Roy was 'banished' to the first floor where he had his own set of rooms! From the age of sixty-seven Roy devoted himself to painting pictures and was still painting well into his eighties.

His work was exhibited in 1981 at the Lancaster City Museum's art exhibition - 'A Century's Span'. William and Roy's years as artists exceeded one hundred years.

Although Roy produced a number of oil and watercolour pictures, it is his etchings, drypoints and pen and ink drawings for which he is better known. He died 16th June 1987 and his ashes are interred in the churchyard at Dorney.

When Iain Dodgson's family 'Studio Arts Gallery' held its special exhibition of Woodhouse work in 1990, featuring both father and son, there were three pencil drawings and fourteen drypoint etchings by Roy. They were mostly 'dog portraiture' at which Roy excelled.

NB.
'Drypoint – engraving technique where the design is 'cut' directly into the bare copper plate using a needle-like instrument called a burin.'

'Etch – reproduce a picture by cutting into a metal plate using acids or corrosives, especially for the purpose of printing copies. An Etching is a copy or print 'taken' from an etched plate'.

The two techniques give a subtly different feel to the resulting image. The drypoint tends to present richer velvet-like lines. This is due to the printing ink being caught in the 'burr' of the engraved line where the metal is lifted to the edges of the line by the engraving needle, like in a ploughed field. Etchings tend to present hard-edged lines in comparison.

Brookhouse, Caton.
Private collection

St. Margaret's Westminster.
Private collection

Winter Landscape after Louis Apol L Springer.   Watercolour.
Private collection

Sailing Ship and Steam Ship after a painting by William Woodhouse.   Watercolour.
Private collection

Appendix I

Transcript from William Woodhouse's diary of his Near East trip 1889. Transcribed by the late Roy Gudgeon and reproduced courtesy of Lancaster City Museums.

Friday 29th.March 1889.

> Arrived in Cardiff at 7.a.m., had breakfast then went aboard 'Moss Brow SS'. In the afternoon went with Nelson to Penarth, and had tea with Mr.J.Pyman. Went to Cardiff Theatre tonight.

Saturday 30th.March.

> Sailed at 6.30.a.m. Passed Lundy at noon. Fresh breeze.

Sunday 31st.March.

> Fresh breeze, all sail on, shipping heavy seas, pig and pigsty nearly overboard.

Monday 1st.April.

> Heavy swell today, moderate towards evening, strong wind on the quarter, all sail set.

Tuesday 2nd. April.

> Strong fair wind, Topsail set. Passed Finisterre at 4.a.m. Whist, yarns and nap. Oil sketch, Bay of Biscay.

Wednesday 3rd.April.

> Fair wind. Passed the Channel Fleet in afternoon. Sighted Cape St. Vincent at 7.30. & abreast the light at 9.30. Quoits morning.

Thursday 4th.April.

> Moderate breeze, off Cadiz at noon. Passed Trafalgar at 3.30. Saw Tangier (Africa) and made watercolour sketch, also Tarifa (Spain) and made sketch. At 5.00. sighted Gibraltar and Ceuta opposite.

Friday 5th.April.

> Passed Cape de Gata at 11 a.m. About a dozen Stormy Petrels follow us all day. Lost one of our laying hens overboard today. Fresh breeze.

Saturday 6th.April.

> Very stormy, W.S.W.wind. Saw the coast of Algiers at 3.p.m. Seas sweeping the decks all day. Whist at night.

Sunday 7th.April.

A fine lazy day, very warm. Reading in the morning and bed in the
afternoon. Africa coast in sight.

Monday 8th.April.

Very fine. Up at 7.30. to sketch Zembra Island and Cape Bon, on the
coast of Tunis (Africa). Quoits on the Quarter deck. We have a
chase after a yellow bird which flew from one end of the ship to the
other, and then left us. In the afternoon another wagtail and a
hawk came, but the sailors on the yard prevented them from
alighting. Passed Pantelleria Island at 3.p.m. Fine moonlight
night.

Tuesday 9th.April 1889

Passed Malta 3.p.m. Fine and fair wind, all sail set. Saw the
first swallow today. A beautiful moonlight night.

Wednesday 10th.April.

Fresh breeze. Sketching until 2 o'clock. Since we left Gibraltar
we lose 20 minutes each day. Several swallows came aboard today and
alighted within a yard of me. Since Monday we have not seen land,
and shall not see any until we arrive at Port Said on Saturday.
Distance from Cardiff to Port Said 3187 miles, 1916 from Gibraltar
to Port Said.

Thursday 11th.April.

Very fine and light breezes. Sketching all morning. In bed
afternoon, sun very powerful. In the evening very pleasant and we
stay on deck until about 8 o'clock. Clear, moonlight and calm.

Friday 12th.April.

We have a sweepstake today on what time we shall arrive in Port
Said, 1/- each. The water in the Mediterranean is quite as blue as
I ever saw it painted, but as we get nearer to the Egyptian coast it
is a muddy green. Fine and light breeze.

Saturday 13th.April.

Passed Rosetta Light at 2.30.a.m. Saw the coast of Egypt at
daylight and Damietta at 10.a.m. We had some good sport this
morning shooting and trying to harpoon large Grampus under the bow
of the ship; some of them were ten or twelve feet long and as many
as four jump out of the water together sending the spray in our
faces. I shot one and they left us for about half an hour and they
came back again; we then tried to harpoon them but did not succeed
and after trying a few times we went off. There are plenty of
Shearwater about, but we did not shoot any, as we could not pick
them up having no landing net. We sighted Port Said about 2 o'clock
and the pilot came on to take charge of the ship.

After tea we get ashore. It is a beautiful moonlight night and the shops are kept open until midnight. About nine o'clock we take a donkey ride down to Arab town, which is about a mile away. My donkey led the way in a gallop and came in first both ways. The town (Arab) consists of a lot of huts and shantys whitewashed which look pretty. The women are dressed in all colours of the rainbow. The houses in Port Said are very pretty in colour and made of cement or wood, with verandahs. I think we can get some good sketches here.

Sunday 14th.April.

Sunday here is almost the same as our Sunday, and it is almost impossible to remember the day. I did not go ashore until after dinner, but after that I made several sketches and purchases. We go aboard rather early as we intend shooting on Lake Manzala tomorrow.

Monday 15th.April 1889.

Up at 5 o'clock. Find our Arab and boat waiting to take us up the Canal as far as the lake, where we hired two more to take us to the island in Lake Manzala. Nelson and Hedley go along the beach and I coast along with the boat. I get some good birds. A White Egret or Stork, one Avocet, three Caspian Terns and one Wild Duck (Pochard). Hedley got a Buzzard, a Sandpiper and two Gulls, and got two shots at Flamingo but missed them. Nelson got four Avocets, one B.B.Gull, one Kentish Plover, a Sandpiper and a Crested Duck. Eighteen birds altogether.
The coast here is very picturesque, camels, mules and arab horses of all kinds and much game and animal life. I shall come and sketch them tomorrow. We saw a good many Pelican and Flamingo, but could not get near them. Got some shells along the beach. This afternoon spent in skinning and curing the birds. After tea we go ashore again, to spend the evening. Bought Tiger skin, Persian Saddle bag, Peacock fans, Crocodile etc.

Tuesday 16th.April.

Boat upset last night with four of our crew and they all manage to scramble out. I went to sketch the Camels working on the Suez Canal; got about twenty sketches. Afternoon to the Cattle Market and I get sketches of cattle, sheep, goats, buffalo etc.

Wednesday 17th.April.

Sketching camels, buffalo etc. in the Arab Market. Many large ships pass through the Canal today, one a Russian convict ship with convicts for Siberia. Several emigrant ships.

Thursday 18th.April.

Sketching most of the time as this is our last day here. We expect to sail about 5 o'clock in the morning. Saw a boat with live turtles on deck. They are found along this coast and are good to see in calm weather.

Friday 19th.April. (Good Friday)

Sailed from Port Said at 7.30. this morning. Light breeze, hazy.
Had two shots at a Buzzard Hawk which hovered over the ship and
missed it, saw several turtle doves and a small hawk. (a flock of
about 150 Pelicans flew across our bow but were too far off to shoot
at). Wind freshening towards evening.

Saturday 20th.April.

Fresh wind but fine, wind still increasing.

Sunday 21st.April. (Easter Sunday).

Blowing very hard this morning and wind ahead. So we make no
headway and are drifting to leeward, no land in sight. Ought to
have seen it on Saturday night at 8 p.m., everything has to be
fastened down, as the ship rolls fearfully and the screw flies round
making an awful row every time the ship plunges (half speed).

Monday 22nd.April 1889.

Land ahead this morning, we are close under the Island of Scarpanto
with Rhode Island to the east in the distance. Just entering the
Grecian Archipelago; Islands of Piscopi, Nisiros, Mandraki, Kos,
Kinaros, Levintha, Leros, Patmos, Nikaria. Tonight it is fine and
calm. The steamer 'Cadoxton' which left Port Said a few hours after
us, is going to overtake us tonight, as she is only about two miles
astern.

Tuesday 23rd. April.

Fine light breeze. 'Cadoxton' passed us in the night. Passed
Islands of Khios and Psara midnight. This morning we are under the
Island of Mytilene once on the mainland of Asia Minor. We have
passed two steamers since sunset. Shearwater are very plentiful
here, flying about in flocks of about thirty. Passed the Island of
Tenedos at 12.a.m. The town and forts of Tenedos are very pretty.
I try to sketch them as we pass. We are close to the Dardanelles
now. Three of us have a bath on the quarter deck with the hose
pipe. Entered the Dardanelles at 12.30. The straits are very
narrow and we can see the people at work with camels and ploughing
with oxen. Made a watercolour sketch of the Dardanelles and we
arrive Gallipoli at 4.45. We are close to the shore and pass very
quickly. This is the prettiest place I have seen for a long time,
and I should like to go ashore. We are now entering the Sea of
Marmara. Sunset, into the Bosphorus at 4.a.m. and Constantinople at
5.a.m.

Wednesday 24th.April.

Up early to sketch Constantinople by sunrise. Go ashore about
9.a.m. We are leaving the ship 'Moss Brow' and intend waiting for
another ship the 'Lizzie English', which left Taganrog in Russia two
days before, and we expect her here tomorrow. We take all our
luggage ashore, and have all our things man-handled by the Customs

Officers, who take all the tobacco they can find and about 200
cartridges. We could not tell a word they say, and we are entirely
at their mercy, and it cost us about 15/- to get it ashore. The
people here think you are made of money, and ask about three times
the value of things for sale. Spent most time today sketching
buffalo and bullock carts which throng the narrow rough paved
streets and dogs which lie about the streets by the score, and
everybody walks around them. A dog here can have a quiet sleep in
the crowded road without being disturbed. Tonight the dogs bark so
much that it is impossible to sleep and at midnight there seemed to
be a score fighting under my bedroom window. An old watchman here
is a great nuisance rattling his stick on the pavement through the
night to frighten away robbers. The dogs here have no owners, about
a dozen of them will take a certain district or corner, and if they
leave that they fight. They are of a tawny colour and very much
resemble the Jackal Wolf or Hyena. Some have their ears pointed
like the wolf and some are cut, others have their ears cut off
altogether.

Thursday 25th.April.1889.

The 'Lizzie English' has not arrived yet, as there has been a fog in
the Black Sea, so we shall not leave here today. Went to the
Stamboul bazaar; got some Turkey carpet squares, saddlebags and
wolfskins. Went to Peta at night. At 10.30.a.m. we took a trip up
the Bosphorus by pleasure steamer as far as the Black Sea. I should
think there is no prettier place anywhere than the Bosphorus, very
picturesque.

Friday 26th.April.

Up at 6.30. this morning and go out sketching. The streets are very
narrow and it is difficult to do anything during the day without a
great crowd. I don't mind the crowd, but they block my view and I
have to pack up. I can't work in the streets more than five minutes
before there are about from twenty to fifty. The 'Lizzie English'
came in last night, and the captain (Findlay) came ashore about
10.30. Went to Stamboul to sketch a Mosque and to get a few
sketches before going aboard. Back to the hotel at 12.30. We go
aboard at 2.30. and sailed at 3.p.m. The sea dead calm through the
Bosphorus and down the Sea of Marmara, arrived in the Dardanelles at
daylight this morning (27th.April).

Saturday 27th.April.

Shot a rare bird in the rigging of the ship this morning. The
breeze is very strong this morning, but we get a little shelter as
we are amongst the Grecian Isles again. Coming down the Sea of
Marmara we saw a flock of about fifty storks about 150 yards off.
Kites and buzzard are plentiful here and a porpoise and grampian go
in shoals of thirty or forty all through the Dardanelles and
Bosphorus. Shearwater pass up and down the narrow straits
continuously in hundreds, but we are not allowed to shoot close to
Constantinople. The country is very fertile and game of all kinds,
from Wild Boar and Deer to Quail abound. We might have seen the
Sultan today if we had cared to do so, but did not take the trouble

to go, but we saw the troops pass on their way to the Palace to
escort him to the Church. It is holiday time here as the Sultan
gets another wife. He takes one every year. The horses and wagons
are very picturesque, they have adopted the Russian harness etc.
since the War. We like our new quarters in the 'Lizzie English'
very well. She is one of 'Pyman's' boats, and is very similar to
'Moss Brow', and everything is very comfortable and clean. She has
been to Mariupol in the Azov and is laden with grain, but is bound
for Bremerhaven up the Weser in Germany. So it is rather awkward
for us; we trust we can be put off at Dover, which the Captain
thinks he can, if the weather is fine and its daylight. If not we
shall go to Bremerhaven and try and get a ship to Hull or
Hartlepool, or if our ship goes to England for orders after
discharging cargo at Bremerhaven, we shall stay a few days there and
land in an English port. We dread changing as we have so much
luggage. We have a dog from Constantinople which Crockford bought
and it just takes him all his time to look after it. The Captain
had bought three turkeys and a pig in Mariupol, but the pig took a
walk through a port-hole just before reaching Constantinople, and
one of the turkeys flew overboard.

Sunday 28th.April 1889.

Fine morning. Strong breeze. Passed the Island of Andros and
through the Gulf of Athens near the ancient city this morning, then
island of Idhra and Spetsai Island, mainland of Greece in sight.
This we can see for many miles. Turtle Dove flew aboard this
morning, but did not stay long enough for us to catch it. Passed
Cape Malea 3.p.m. Saw the hermit who lives there. We are now going
through Kithirai Channel. Cerigotto Island is on the south side.
The wind has increased very much today and it is now blowing very
hard, spray flying over the bridge at times. Stormy night.

Monday 29th.April.

Roused up early this morning by the Captain bringing in a Quail
which he caught on deck, and said there was a Turtle Dove on the
fore deck. I went out just in time to see one of the sailors
attempt to catch it but failed. A good many Quail visited us today,
one of which I shot but it fell overboard. There is less wind this
morning and it gradually falls away towards night. We expect to
arrive in Malta tomorrow about 4 o'clock. Made three watercolour
sketches this morning, one of the Constantinople dog, Engineer' dog,
and portrait of the Captain. Skinned and preserved the Quail.
Played nap this afternoon with Captain, Nelson and Crockford.

Tuesday 30th.April.

Fine morning breeze, very light. Several Turtle doves visited us
today, also swallows and yellow wagtail. Nelson caught one of the
swallows with his hand. Several Grampus sped under the bows of the
ship. Sighted Malta about 4.p.m. Malta is the island where St.Paul
was wrecked. One Bay is called St Paul's Bay, there is also
St.Paul's Church and several other places named after St.Paul. We
went ashore after tea and had a good look around. The buildings
here are much more substantial and much cleaner than other places we

have visited, and we get on better here as they speak English. We
leave Crockford here, but another young fellow joins us here for
England. Went to St.John's Church. We sailed again this Tuesday
night. The warships 'Edinburgh', 'Dolphin', 'Hibernia' (old wooden
ship), 'Temerain', 'Benbow' and several gunboats are lying in the
harbour. We pass the place tonight where the 'Sultan' is wrecked.

Wednesday 1st.May.

Very fair morning, light breeze. Several birds visited us today.
Doves, Hawks, Nightjars etc. Sighted the Island of Pantelleria
about 11.a.m. and Cape Bon on African coast at 4.30.p.m. Passed
several sailing vessels, fair wind. Tonight the sky is overcast and
threatens rain.

Thursday 2nd.May.

Grey morning, a little rain during the night but clear at noon
again. Passed the 'Dog Rocks' at 10.p.m. last night and Galite at
8.a.m. today. Two Quail came to the ship but dropped in the water.
Nelson shot a Turtle Dove and I caught a yellow wagtail.   A few
swallows came aboard tonight and perch under the bulwark, we could
easily take them if we wished, but did not disturb them. Nap on
deck this afternoon. Raining heavily at 11.p.m.

Friday 3rd.May 1889.

Fine and very warm. Large shoals of Grampus spout about, the water
is alive with them, I went to look over the bows and saw about
twenty just in front almost touching the ship. Passed Algiers at
4.p.m. We are yet two days sail from Gibraltar. We expect to see
the Spanish coast tomorrow. Fair night, new moon.

Saturday 4th.May.

Fine morning, fresh breeze. This has been rather a long day as we
have seen no ships, birds, porpoises or anything. Spent the morning
working on a Constantinople sketch of buffalo. We can see Cape de
Gata (Spain) tonight, which is about 150 miles from Gibraltar and
expect to be there tomorrow evening. Four or five days sail now is
beginning to be rather trying to us all and we are quite ready for
the opportunity to go ashore. We are liable to be put in quarantine
for a week here through not having had a bill of health from Malta,
but manage to get it squared.

<u>Sunday 5th.May</u>.

Fair strong breeze. We are sailing all day along the south coast of
Spain, the tops of the higher hills are covered with snow. Sighted
the Rock of Gibraltar about 2.p.m. arrived at 7.p.m. We take in 180
tons of coal here, so we shall stay until midnight. After the
quarantine flag is taken down we are permitted to go ashore in the
small steam launch which is waiting for the Captain. We go and see
the town and make a few purchases and go aboard at 10.p.m. The
people here are English, Spanish, Moors and Maltese. Today is a
feast day or holiday, all dress in their best. Expect to sail at
1.a.m.

<u>Monday 6th.May</u>.

Very strong breeze today from the West. Chief mate saw a Whale
today but the sea being rough he soon lost sight of it. We were
below at the time. Saw a large shoal of porpoise. A small bird
flew aboard this morning but it died almost immediately it alighted.
We shall round Cape St.Vincent about midnight, and ought to see the
light now, 10.30.p.m., but it is too cold tonight to look for lights
and we turn in. See many steamers and ships today.

<u>Tuesday 7th.May</u>.

Grey morning, light wind. Passed Cape St.Vincent 2.a.m. Cape Roche
about noon and Berlengas Island 7.p.m. Rather foggy night.

<u>Wednesday 8th.May</u>.

Very strong breeze. Got no sleep last night. The whistle was going
all night, and we go half speed through the fog, but it is clear
this morning, but stormy. We passed Cape Finisterre about 2.a.m.
and are now fairly in the Bay of Biscay again. Wind increasing
through the day and tonight the sea is running fearfully high and
sweeping the decks. I turn in rather earlier as we can do nothing
but hold on; got no sleep.

<u>Thursday 9th.May 1889</u>.

Sea running very high this morning. We have all sail on, and wind
on the starboard quarter, which has made her list very much, and our
cargo has shifted so that she scarcely gets upright at all. Tons of
water come over us, and completely smothers the ship at times. We
are now about the middle of the bay. The Chief Engineer threatens
to stop the ship if the cargo is not put right as it is almost
impossible to do anything down below by the engineers or firemen.
Our lee rail is under water very often. 7.p.m. All sail is taken
in, an attempt is made to put the cargo right, and the ship is
stopped and turned south into the wind. Heavy chains are packed to
windward, but before they were secured the ship was started again,
which threw the chains weighing several tons, over the men at work.
They threaten they won't go below again. One man was hurt very much
but will soon be right again. 8.p.m. The wind is a little lighter
and we go on again but every half hour or so comes two or three

tremendous waves which almost turn us over. I go to bed early and
read, then try to sleep towards midnight but cannot, this is the
third night I get no sleep. I can't turn over in bed, as I was
thrown violently against the cabin side this afternoon when the ship
lurched, and hurt my right thigh so badly that I dare not sleep on
it. I shall be glad when we are across the bay.

Friday 10th.May.

Not quite so bad this morning. The wind has come more astern, and
the men who are shifting cargo have succeeded in making it a little
better, but we still have a heavy list. The engineer had worked
about eighteen tons of coal from the lower side bunkers which makes
much difference. The wind is lighter but the sea has not gone down
much. If we can only go on as we are we shall make the French coast
(Ushant) tonight about 12 o'clock. A whale is spouting to windward
sending the water about twenty feet high every time it blows. I
watched it for a long time before I lost sight of it. Lots of
Kittiwake are about this morning which looks as if we are nearing
home. We never saw any further south. Sighted Ushant light on the
French coast at 8.p.m. Fair night and wind gone down.

Saturday 11th.May.

Fine morning, dead calm. Off the Channel Isles and Caskets about
10.a.m. We expect to be off Dover tomorrow morning and if we can
get off there we will do so. Off the Isle of Wight at 5.p.m.
Packed up ready for leaving in the morning if possible.

Sunday 12th.May.

Passed Beachey Head at 4.a.m., Dover 8.a.m. The wind has risen
during the night which would make it difficult to land, and it is
raining fast. We are rather a long way from the shore and there are
no boats about. So we go on to Bremerhaven. Passed a few Dutch and
English fishing boats. Raining most part of the day. Its coming
down heavily just now, 10.p.m.

Monday 13th.May.1889.

Fine morning, light breeze. I was up early, 5.a.m. to see a large
fleet of fishing boats, English and Dutch and get sketches. In the
Texel Islands (the first of the Frisian Group) early this morning,
and dropped anchor in the River Weser at 7.30.p.m. We will go up to
Bremerhaven with the morning tide. There is not much water here,
but the place is well buoyed, lighted and there are plenty of
pilots, we took our pilot up at 1.a.m. Lots of wildfowl here and we
saw a good many duck. Crane shaft fell overboard, weighing about
two tons, had to anchor to get it aboard, great excitement. A rat
hunt on deck tonight. We will try and get a boat at Bremerhaven for
Hull. The pilot says that two boats a week sail from here
(passenger) so when we get off tomorrow, we will look out for one to
take us across the North Sea. Distance to Hull about 350 miles
which will occupy one and a half days.

Tuesday 14th.May.

    Arrived in Bemerhaven at noon and take our luggage ashore.

Wednesday 15th.May.

    Sailed from Bremerhaven in the North German Lloyd Steamer 'Trave' for Southampton and arrived in Southampton 3.p.m. Thursday 16th. Being delayed by fog.

Thursday 16th.May.

    Left Southampton for London 7.25. arrived in London 10.p.m.

Friday 17th.May.

    Academy.

Saturday 18th.May.

    Left London. 1.15.p.m.

Appendix II

WILLIAM WOODHOUSE – Exhibitions.   (1881 to date)

Where known, the year and exhibition/catalogue number precedes the title of the painting, followed by the sale price if appropriate. Where relevant, extra information has been added in italics.

Circa 1881   **A Lancaster Exhibition held at The Mechanic's Institute, Lancaster.**

        102   A Cottage.   7 guineas

        410   Calf Love.   £30

        (This was possibly the first time that Woodhouse's paintings were shown at an exhibition)

1883   **Royal Scottish Academy Exhibition**

        566   Oxen at Rest.

        (William's address for this exhibition was 10 Queens Terrace, Morecambe)

1889   **Royal Academy**

        Doomed. *(See chapter on R.A. exhibits)*

1889   **Institute of Painters in Oils**

        Horseplay.   £50

        (This painting was reproduced by The Fine Arts Co. Ltd. London)

1894   **The Second Annual Art Exhibition of Pictures in Oils and Watercolours**
Municipal Art Gallery, Storey Institute, Lancaster.

        16th June to 15th September, 1894.

        8   Oxen at Rest   £15

        65   Wounded Wapiti   £ 12   10s

        76   First Steps in Life   £ 8

        138   The Sweeping Blast of Sky O'ercast
                the Joyous Winter Day   £15

1895   **The Third Annual Art Exhibition of Pictures in Oils and Watercolours**
Municipal Art Gallery, Storey Institute, Lancaster.

        8th July to 21st September, 1895.

        44   The Bath.   *(Oil)*   12 guineas.

        81   Setters.   *(Oil)*   £20

        142 Waiting for Master.   *(Oil)*   £14 10s

(The Lancaster Guardian, July 1895 noted that Woodhouse had secured a prominent position for his admirable picture of 'Setters'; the animals were splendidly drawn and coloured. An equally powerful painting was 'Waiting for Master' representing a spaniel and terrier at the door of a keeper's cottage listening intently for the sound of master's footsteps)

1896 **Royal Academy**
Wolves and Wild Boar.
(See chapter on R.A. exhibits)

1896 **Derby Corporation Art Gallery**
Wolves and Wapiti.   £25
(Described by Woodhouse as a Big Game Subject)

1896 **Royal Birmingham Society of Artists Exhibition**
Bison and Wolves.   £25

1908 **Lancaster Exhibition**, **Storey Institute, Lancaster.**
Consisted of 11 oils and 4 watercolours:
Oil Paintings:
Borwick Hall.
Chillingham Cattle.
The Close of Day.   9 guineas
First Steps.   *(puppies)*
Fox Hunting.
Gone Away.   9 guineas
Horse and Groom.
The Hunted Stag.   39 guineas
Kittens and Mouse.
Mare and Foal.
Terrors of the Prairie.   20 guineas

Watercolours:
Carting the Seaweed.
Haymaking.
Heysham Village.
Old Russian Barque.
(This was the Vanadis, which was wrecked in Half Moon Bay, Heysham in 1903)

(Only four of the above paintings were for sale, the others belonged to a private collector)

1911 **Royal Academy**
Vanquished. *(See chapter on R.A. exhibits)*

1911   **Royal Institute of Painters in Watercolours**
Battleship Raleigh - lying at its last anchorage in the hands of its destroyers.
(Ward's Ship Breakers Yard)

A Battery of Horse at Bare Camp.
(Bare Camp was a military training ground where soldiers spent two weeks training during the summer. For example in 1900 the Keighley Volunteers trained there, as did the Second West Yorkshire Battalion Field Artillery in 1908)

1925   **Royal Institute of Painters in Watercolours**

1926   **Southport – 41st Spring Exhibition of Modern Art at the Atkinson Art Gallery**
26th April to 26th June 1926
241   Discussing the Weight.   £26 5s.
(Featuring a recently shot stag about to be weighed. This painting appeared at other exhibitions and became quite well known, although it never sold and was eventually retained in the Woodhouse family collection)

Appendix III

Exhibitions at the Harris Museum and Art Gallery, Preston.

Catalogues which included work by William Woodhouse.

1926	**Copies of the catalogue for the First Annual Spring Exhibition are missing.**	

1927   **The Second Annual Spring Exhibition of Paintings by Lancashire Artists**
March 31st to May 4th, 1927.

| 107 | In the Great Lone Land. | £26 5s 0d. |
| 108 | Discussing the Weight. | £26 5s 0d. |

1928   **The Third Annual Spring Exhibition of Paintings by Lancashire Artists**
March 29th to May 5th, 1928.

146	Woodcock and Snipe.	£8 18s 6d.
147	Cormorant and Rogor Bills. (sic)	£8 18s 6d.
148	Waterhen and Snipe.	£8 18s 6d.

1929   **The Fourth Annual Spring Exhibition of Pictures by Lancashire Artists**
March 28th to May 4th, 1929.

181	Woodcock.	£ 8 8s 0d.
182	Green Plover.	£15 15s 0d.
183	Partridge.	£ 8 8s 0d.

1930   **The Fifth Annual Spring Exhibition of Pictures by Lancashire Artists**
April 10th to May 17th, 1930.

99	Snipe.	£ 8 8s 0d.
104	Capercaille. *(A kind of Grouse)*	£ 8 8s 0d.
128	Moose.	£15 15s 0d.

(After this exhibition the Harris Art Gallery purchased the painting of 'Snipe', which is in their art collection)

1931   **The Sixth Annual Spring Exhibition of Pictures by Lancashire Artists**
March 26th to May 9th, 1931.

109	Heysham Baulks.	£ 8 8s 0d.
218	Capercaille.	£15 15s 0d.
270	Woodcock.	£ 8 8s 0d.

1932   **The Seventh Annual Spring Exhibition of Works by Lancashire Artists**

March 17th to April 30th, 1932.

109	Great Cormorant.	
194	Gannets, Ailsa Craig.	
198	Kittiwakes, Farne Islands.	

1933   **The Eighth Annual Spring Exhibition of Works by Lancashire Artists**

March 24th to April 29th, 1933.

| 125 | Kestrel. | £ 8 8s 0d. |
| 136 | Fieldfares. | £ 8 8s 0d. |

1934   **The Ninth Annual Spring Exhibition of Works by Lancashire Artists**

March 22nd to April 28th, 1934.

170	The Deerstalker's Pony.	£ 8 8s 0d.
171	H.M.S. Akbar.	£15 15s 0d.
173	Woodcock.	£ 8 8s 0d.

1935   **The Tenth Annual Spring Exhibition of Work by Lancashire Artists**

March 28th to April 27th, 1935.

216	Waterhen.	£ 8 8s 0d.
240	Snipe.	£ 8 8s 0d.
252	Channock - Dardanelles.	£ 8 8s 0d.

1936   **The Eleventh Annual Spring Exhibition of Work by Lancashire Artists**

March 26th to April 25th, 1936.

| 105 | Jungle Friends. | £ 8 8s 0d. |
| 117 | The Wanderers. | £ 8 8s 0d. |

1937   **The Twelfth Annual Spring Exhibition of Work by Lancashire Artists**

11th March to April 10th, 1937.

| 51 | Indian Big Game. | |
| 68 | Hard Pressed. | |

1938   **Catalogues for the Thirteenth Annual Spring Exhibition are missing.**

1939   The Fourteenth Annual Spring Exhibition of Lancashire Art

16th March to April 15th, 1939.

(A Memorial Exhibition of Works by William Woodhouse was included in this Exhibition)

88	Mallard.
89	Bolton Abbey, Yorks.
90	Pheasant.
91	Polar Bear and Seals.
92	Borwick Hall.
93	Puffins.
94	Study.
95	The Stack Yard.
96	Rhino and Tiger.
97	Wild Duck.
98	Woodcock and Heron.
99	Pheasants.
100	Otter and Pike.
101	Barn Owl.
102	The Wanderers.
103	Osprey.
104	Bittern.
105	Woodcock and Snipe.
106	Squirrcls.
107	Jungle Friends.
108	Pheasant.
109	Capercaillie.
110	Going to the Horse Fair.
111	H.M.S. Akbar.
112	Buffalo.
113	The Mosque Steps.
114	Grouse in Winter.
115	Mergansers.
116	Landscape.
117	Mallards in Flight.
118	Widgeon.
119	Scene in Spain.
120	Hooded Crows.
121	The Sportsman.
122	Portrait of Charles Dickens[1].
123	At Sea.
124	Circus Rider.
125	Camel Study.
126	Teal in Winter.
127	Landscape Sketch.
128	The Blacksmith.
129	A Sunny Corner.
130	Landscape Sketch.

Paintings sold at Exhibition:

98	Woodcock and Heron.	12 guineas.
117	Mallards in Flight.	£5 0s 0d.
121	The Sportsman.	2 guineas.
129	A Sunny Corner.	4 guineas.
134	The Old Reaper.	4 guineas.
140	The Woodcutters.	£5 0s 0d.
147	The Old Willows.	£4 0s 0d.
156	The Wild Fowler.	5 guineas.
160	Resting.	4 guineas.
163	Dog Study.	2 guineas.
166	The White Horse.	1 guinea.
176	Study of A Horse.	2 guineas.

(After the exhibition the Harris Art Gallery purchased):

161	Lapwing.	*(See Bird Paintings)*
174	Study of a Horse.	*(See Horse Paintings)*
175	Horse and Foal.	*(See Horse Paintings)*

(All three paintings remain in their art collection)

Notes

No.1   *Portrait of Charles Dickens (1812-1870). It is known that Charles Dickens visited Lancaster with his friend Wilkie Collins on a number of occasions and stayed at the Old Kings Arms Hotel, where Joseph Sly was licensee. Dickens and Sly appear to have struck up a friendship and corresponded with one another for a number of years. It is not known if William Woodhouse met Charles Dickens, however Woodhouse did become friendly with Joseph Sly's grandson (also Joseph) as he married my grandfather's sister, Florence Hogarth.*

1940   **The Fifteenth Annual Spring Exhibition of Lancashire Art**
13th March to 15th April 1940.

285	Head of Bull	(Watercolour)	9 guineas.
307	Collie	(Watercolour)	8 guineas.
320	Spaniel and Mallard	(Watercolour)	10 guineas.

1943   **The Eighteenth Annual Spring Exhibition of Lancashire Art**
24th March to 26th April 1943.

| 429 | The Badger | (Watercolour) | 6 guineas. |
| 439 | Oystercatcher | (Watercolour) | 6 guineas. |

1944   **The Nineteenth Annual Spring Exhibition of Lancashire Art**
15th March to 22nd April 1944.

| 375 | Hares. | (Watercolour) | 14 guineas. |
| 385 | Moose | (Watercolour) | 14 guineas. |

1949   **Twenty-fourth Annual Spring Exhibition of Lancashire Art**
16th March to 18th April (Easter Monday) 1949.

| 42 | Game | | 4 guineas. |
| 97 | Port Said | | 7 guineas. |

1927   **Loan Exhibition of Paintings**
             Harris Museum and Art Gallery - Preston
             5th December to 31st December 1927.

Oil paintings:		**Paintings sold**
1	Dog and Pheasant.	18 guineas
2	Spaniel and Wild Duck.	
3	Cattle Crossing Morecambe Sands.	15 guineas
4	Fell Ponies.	

Watercolours:		
5	Going to the Horse Fair.	
6	Pheasants Rising.	
7	Waterhen and Snipe. *(Sold)*	
8	Golden Eagle.	
9	Barn Owl.	
10	Otter and Pike.	
11	Cormorants.	
12	Pheasants.	14 guineas
13	Flighting Time.	
14	H.M.S.Akbar.	
15	Squirrels.	
16	Partridge Drive.	8 guineas
17	Near Bolton Abbey.	8 guineas
18	A Hunting Morning.	
19	Devil's Bridge, Kirkby Lonsdale.	8 guineas
20	Linton Falls, Yorks.	£7
21	River Wharfe, near Stepping Stones.	£7
22	Pheasant Shooting, 1820.	
23	Barden Moors.	
24	Cuckoo.	
25	Blackcock.	
26	Grouse Driving, Barden Moors.	
27	The Edge of the Cover.	
28	Pheasant and Setter.	8 guineas
29	Roebuck and Hounds.	
30	Gannets.	
31	A Shot at the Slaver.	
32	Heysham.	£7
33	Cromwell's Cottage, Edgehill.	
34	May.	£7

35	Drake Goes West.	£8
36	Squirrel.	
37	Off Gibraltar.	
38	Heysham. *(Sold)*	
39	Goldeneye and Widgeon.	
40	Heysham Village.	£7
41	Barque off Piel.	
42	Grouse Shooting.	8 guineas
43	Springtime.	
44	Dutch Craft on River Weser.	
45	Gypsy Camp.	
46	Woodcock. *(Sold)*	
47	Bracken Harvest, Barden Moor.	
48	Falconry.	
49	Mare and Foal.	
50	Haytime.	
51	Pig Sticking.	
52	Return of the Mussel Gatherers.	8 guineas
53	Mussel Carts.	
54	A Sea Dog.	
55	Snow Leopard.	
56	Returning to the Kill.	
57	Outward Bound.	
58	Woodcutters.	8 guineas
59	Gargrave Lock.	
60	Shrimpers.	
61	Pheasant Shooting.	
62	Borwick Hall. *(Not for Sale)*	

Reproductions from Oil Paintings:
63	Winter Fodder.
64	Dancing Bear.
65	Vicar's Tithe.
66	Fodder Gang.
67	Donkeys - Morecambe Sands.
68	The Cottage Door.
69	Setter and French Partridge.
70	Bull.

(No. 63-70 published by the Fine Art Publishing Co., London)

(Preston Corporation bought three watercolours for their permanent Art Collection):
31	A Shot at the Slaver.
55	Snow Leopard.
60	Shrimpers.

Appendix V

1931   **The 9th Lancaster Art Exhibition at the Storey Institute**
9th June – 22nd July 1931.

Oils and Watercolours:

		£	s.	d.
1	Woodcock.	9	9	0
2	Gannets, Ailsa Craig.			
3	Curlew.			
4	Kirkby Lonsdale Bridge.			
5	Borwick Hall in Olden Times.			
6	Old Willows.			
7	Snipe.			
8	Staithes.			
9	Off to the Mussel Skears. (sic)			
10	Clearing the Woodlands.			
11	Bostocks.			
12	Sunderland Point.			
13	Capercailize. (sic)	14	14	0
14	Woodcock.			
15	Capercailize. (sic)			
16	Stag Taking to the Water.			
17	Golden Ball, Snatchems.			
18	Cavalry Horses.			
19	"Majestic".			
20	Pheasant Coming Out of Cover.			
21	Golden Eagle and White Hare.			
22	A Hazy Morning.			
23	Timber Hauling.			
24	Moose.	14	14	0
25	Discussing the Weight.	26	5	0
26	Kirkby Lonsdale Bridge.			
27	Morecambe 70 years Ago. *(After an Old Drawing)*			
28	In the Great Lone Land.	21	0	0
29	The Old Golf Links, Heysham.			
30	A Bend in the Wharfe.			
31	Bolton Woods.			
32	May Blossom.			
33	After Trafalgar.			
34	Going to Market.			
35	Golden Eagle.	18	18	0

36	Study of Head.			
37	Roses.			
38	Portrait.			
39	The Belfry, Bruges.			
40	Constantinople.			
41	Old Harbour, Morecambe.			
42	Stag, Hind, and Fawn.			
43	The Shore, Heysham.			
44	Wood Pigeons.			
45	Grouse.			
46	Spaniel and Woodcock.	14	0	0
47	A Mixed Bag.	20	0	0
48	The Top of the Hill.			
49	Moose at Bay.			
50	Lunch Time.			
51	Flanders Field.			
52	Tiger Hunting.			
53	Spaniel and Mallard.			
54	1914.			
55	Freedom.			
56	Spring Ploughing.			
57	The Bag.			
58	Fell Rangers.			
59	Retrieved.	14	0	0
60	Brace of Sporting Spaniels.			
61	The Deer Pony.			
62	Water-hen and Water-rail.			
63	The Shoeing Forge.			
64	Lobster Fisher.			
65	Portrait.			
66	Head Study. (*After Sir Thomas Lawrence*)			
67	Portrait.			
68	Portrait Group.			
69	Portrait.			
70	The Shore Shooter.			
71	Portrait Group.			
72	Off to His Lair.			
73	Chillingham Cattle.			
74	English and Irish Setters.			
75	The Horse Thresher.			
76	Wild Duck Shooting.	14	0	0
77	Spaniel and Widgeon.			
78	The Hunted Stag.	42	0	0
79	Trespassers.	21	0	0
80	Crossing the Lancaster Sands - Olden Times.			
81	Black Game.			

82	The Timber Wagon.			
83	Orvar.			
84	The Groom.			
85	The Smithy.			
86	Brookhouse Village.			
87	A Quiet Cove.	7	7	0
88	The Road to the Shore.			
89	Crossing the Channel, 1914.	21	0	0
90	The Village Pump, Heysham.	6	0	0
91	The Manor House, Embsay.			
92	Polar Bear and Seal.			
93	Evening.			
94	Young Bull.	15	15	0
95	Study of Head.			
96	Sheep.			
97	Wild Boars.	6	6	0
98	Feeding Time.			
99	Sportsman's Companion.			
100	Knipe's Orchard.			
101	Vanquished.	31	10	0
102	Tiger and Cubs.	6	6	0
103	A Hot Scent.			
104	Drawing the Spinney.			
105	Leopards.			
106	Wild Duck.	20	0	0
107	Lancaster Marsh.			
108	Bambro' Castle.			
109	Buffalo Resting.			
110	Wagon Horse, Old Jetty, Morecambe.			
111	Hunting.			
112	Scotch Cattle.			
113	Tiger - The Jungle.			
114	Early Morning at the Circus.			
115	The Attack.	20	0	0
116	The White Horse Inn Banbury.			
117	Cocker Spaniel.	20	0	0
118	Grouse Shooting.	10	10	0
119	Landscape with Cattle. *(After Bercham)*			
120	Fox.			
121	The Lights of Peace.			
122	Waiting for Help.			
123	St. Patricks.	9	9	0
124	Waiting for the Mussel Boats, Morecambe.			
125	Mussel Carts.			
126	A Small Holding.			
127	The Donkey Boy.	31	10	0

128	Evening Pastures.			
129	Red Riding Hood.			
130	The Stackyard.	8	8	0
131	Hest Bank Canal.	8	8	0
132	Teal.			
133	A Hunting Morning.	8	8	0
134	Obsolete.	8	8	0
135	Heysham Baulks.	8	8	0
136	Partridge.	8	8	0
137	Canadian Moose.	8	8	0
138	Seraglio Point, Constantinople.	8	8	0
139	Ptarmigan.	6	6	0
140	Green Plover.	14	14	0
141	On the Bosphorus.	8	8	0
142	A Game Cover Side.	8	8	0
143	Roe Deer.	8	8	0
144	Entrance to the Black Sea.	8	8	0
145	Sea-Pies.	8	8	0
146	Ship in Tow.	8	8	0
147	Woodcock.	8	8	0
148	The Pond.	8	8	0
149	The Canal.	8	8	0
150	St. Patrick's Ruins, Heysham.	8	8	0
151	A Country Lane.	8	8	0
152	Newby Bridge.	8	8	0
153	Wood Pigeons.	8	8	0
154	Woodcock and Snipe.	8	8	0
155	Gargrave Lock.	8	8	0
156	Haytime.	6	6	0
157	Falconry.	8	8	0
158	Otter and Pike.	14	14	0
159	An Old World Village.	8	8	0
160	Shoveller Ducks.	8	8	0
161	Pig Sticking.	8	8	0
162	A Heysham Farm.	8	8	0
163	Marsh Farm.	8	8	0
164	The Gleaners.	8	8	0
165	Barn Owl.	14	14	0
166	Widgeon Shooting.	8	8	0
167	Merganser and Scaup.	8	8	0
168	Dutch Fishers.	8	8	0
169	Wooden Walls.			
170	The Light Ship.	8	8	0
171	Kittiwakes.	8	8	0
172	The Badger.	8	8	0
173	Mussel Gatherers.	8	8	0

174	Squirrels at Play.	14	14	0
175	The Great Cormorant.	8	8	0
176	Beaten from Cover.	14	14	0
177	Blackcock.	8	8	0
178	Pheasants.	14	14	0
179	An Old Time Sportsman.	8	8	0
180	Grey Duck.	14	14	0
181	Shovellers.	8	8	0
182	Sable Antelope.	8	8	0
183	Haunts of the Great Cormorant.	14	14	0
184	The Old Moat Skipton.	8	8	0
185	A Rocky Point, Heysham.	8	8	0
186	Cumberland Hills.	8	8	0
187	Roses.	6	6	0
188	An Old Salt.	6	6	0
189	On Embsay Crag.	8	8	0
190	Gibraltar.	8	8	0
191	A Woodland Rambler.	8	8	0

A few of the paintings that the newspaper critics commented upon:

Gannets on Ailsa Craig: "there is a sense of freedom and the clean tang of the sea breeze about this which reflects the artists outdoor personality".

The Devils Bridge at Kirkby Lonsdale: "is quickly recognizable".

Borwick Hall: "the artists imagination has had full sway and the picturesque setting of Borwick Hall is peopled with the figures of a falcon party about to set off for the hunt."

Staithes: "a splendid study of wind tossed 'Staithes' the birth place of Captain Cook".

Off to the Mussel Skears: [sic] "a fine bold picture showing fisherman".

'Bostocks': "as the prosaic title of a study showing circus animals - ponies and an elephant feeding from the same truss".

Stag Taking to Water:
(The Hunted Stag). "depicts the Monarch of the woods taking to the sea, closely pursued by the hounds with the huntsmen left at the water's edge"

After Trafalgar: "a fine naval study showing the Victory being towed into Gibraltar after Trafalgar".

Constantinople: "another fine landscape".

Old Harbour Morecambe: "reminiscent of the days when the old jetty of Morecambe was a harbour with a busy scene landing Irish cattle from the boat - Mr. Woodhouse has faithfully presented a phase of activity that has its more modern counterpart at Heysham docks everyday of the week and it is a thrillingly vivid picture".

Fell Rangers: "is the title of an extremely effective subject with three moorland ponies and a hare as the dramatic personae, with a moorland setting that instinctively carries the scent of the heather on the keen breeze".

The Donkey Boy: "in which a familiar figure on Morecambe Sands, stands in attendance on two of his charges".

A Portrait of Mrs. Ellen Hogarth with her Daughter: (Wife of Major Bertram Whewell Hogarth J.P. and their Daughter Joan):   "a life-like picture painted many years ago". (circa 1904-5).

Spring Ploughing: "a well studied sky but it is the horses that have the vitality".

In the Great Lone Land: "a herd of bison surrounded by wolves".

The Attack: "a bison and calf are threatened by wolves, in which the fur is most realistic".

Three paintings of Scottish Game: "a delight to the eye".

Of Interest to Local Visitors: "the windswept willows on the old Morecambe Golf Links".

The Golden Ball, Snatchems: "picturesque hostelry by the side of the Lune".

Canal at Hest Bank   "another charming landscape".

Landscapes depicting various phases of the Craven District, including: "Skipton Castle, and beauty spots in the vicinity of Gargrave".

Among the Drawings one critic picked out: "Roe Deer, Sea-Pies, Otter and Pike, Barn Owl, The Badger, Sable Antelope, as examples of searching animal-life".

Appendix VI

1933 **Exhibition of Oil Paintings & Watercolours by**
William Woodhouse
Heysham former Council Rooms
26th September to 16th October 1933

	Oil Paintings:	£	s.	d.
1	Spaniel and Pheasant.	15	15	0
2	Polar Bear.	Not for Sale		
3	The Troop Ship.	Not for Sale		
4	Portrait Group.	Not for Sale		
5	Spaniel and Wild Duck.	15	15	0
6	Bison and Wolves.	21	0	0
7	Tigress and Cubs.	5	5	0
8	Gun Dogs.	15	15	0
9	Ploughing.	Not for Sale		
10	Held at Bay.	Not for Sale		
11	Retrieving Wild Duck.	Not for Sale		
12	Crossing the Sands.	Not for Sale		
13	Wild Boar.	5	5	0
14	Pigeons.	Not for Sale		
15	Vanquished.	21	0	0
16	Arrival of the Irish Cattle Boat, Morecambe Old Harbour.	Not for Sale		
17	The Hunted Stag.	31	0	0
18	Timber Wagon	Not for Sale		
19	Fell Ponies.	Not for Sale		
20	Black Game.	15	15	0
21	Bringing up the Guns 1914.	Not for Sale		
22	Threshing.	Not for Sale		
23	Portrait Group.	Not for Sale		
24	The Stalker's Pony.	Not for Sale		
25	Spaniel and Rabbits.	15	15	0
26	Charging the Guns, 1914.	Not for Sale		

	Watercolours:			
27	Green Plover.	15	15	0
28	Stranded – (The Old Morecambe Lightship). *(Framed)*	4	4	0
29	Heysham. *(Framed)*	6	6	0
30	Poulton-le-Sands, 1846 - Site of the Central Flagstaff. *(Framed)*	4	4	0
31	Elephants and Egrets.	Not for Sale		
32	Wild Boar Hunting.	7	7	0

33	Cormorants.	8	8	0
34	Stackyard.	8	8	0
35	Quarry Bridge.	4	4	0
36	H.M.S. Akbar in Morecambe old Harbour.	Not for Sale		
37	Badger.	8	8	0
38	Partridge in Stubble.	8	8	0
39	The Baulks.	8	8	0
40	The Scrapyard - H.M.S. Raleigh.	8	8	0
41	Fox.	8	8	0
42	Old Morecambe Front.	8	8	0
43	Merganser.	8	8	0
44	Silverdale Rocks.	7	7	0
45	Roebuck.	Not for Sale		
46	Morecambe Old Lightship.	5	5	0
47	Pheasants.	8	8	0
48	Embsay Moor.	6	6	0
49	Dutch Fishing Boats.	6	6	0
50	Clark's Stackyard.	8	8	0
51	Shoveller Duck.	Not for Sale		
52	Gargrave Lock.	8	8	0
53	Mussel Cart.	8	8	0
54	Heysham Rocks.	8	8	0
55	Silverdale Shore.	5	5	0
56	Capercailzie.	15	15	0
57	The Timber Team.	8	8	0
58	Silverdale.	8	8	0
59	Sable Antelope.	Not for Sale		
60	Pointer and Blackcock.	7	7	0
61	Shelducks.	8	8	0
62	Hornby Bridge.	8	8	0
63	The Bosphorus.	8	8	0
64	Shelducks - Silverdale Marsh.	8	8	0
65	Roebuck.	4	4	0
66	Pheasants.	15	15	0
67	Woodcock.	8	8	0
68	Oystercatchers.	8	8	0
69	The Cove, Silverdale	8	8	0
70	Woodcock and Snipe.	7	7	0
71	Woodpigeons.	7	7	0
72	The Willows - Heysham Old Golf Links.	8	8	0
73	Gibraltar.	8	8	0
74	Falconry Days.	8	8	0
75	Sailing Barge.	5	5	0
76	Cormorants.	15	15	0
77	Pheasants.	8	8	0

78	Seascape.	7	7	0
79	Stamboul, The Bosphorus.	8	8	0
80	Heysham Rocks.	7	7	0
81	Fieldfares.	8	8	0
82	The Bosphorus.	8	8	0
83	The Farne Islands.	8	8	0
84	Squirrel.	8	8	0
85	Otter and Pike.	15	15	0
86	Eagle. *(Framed)*	17	17	0
87	Bempton Cliffs, Flamborough Head.	8	8	0
88	Pheasants.	15	15	0
89	Kestrel.	Not for Sale		
90	Gannets on Ailsa Craig.	Not for Sale		
91	Wigeon.	7	7	0
92	Squirrels.	15	15	0
93	Haytime.	5	5	0
94	Heysham Village, Central.	8	8	0
95	Chillingham Cattle.	Not for Sale		
96	Going to the Fair.	15	15	0
97	Wreck of the Vanadis, Heysham.	7	7	0
98	Pheasant Shooting.	8	8	0
99	Barn Owl.	15	15	0
100	Discussing the Weight. *(Framed)*	21	0	0
101	Turkish Wagon Team. *(Framed)*	4	4	0
102	"Old Jack".	Not for Sale		
103	Heysham, The Old Pump. *(Framed)*	5	5	0
104	The Buffalo Herd. *(Framed)*	21	0	0

Appendix VII

1934   **Oxford Exhibition**
2nd July to 7th July 1934.

1   Woodcock.
2   Snipe.
3   Osprey.
4   Kestrel.
5   Gannets.
6   Fieldfare.

1934   **Bristol Exhibition**
Mid July to Mid August 1934.

(This exhibition followed on from the Oxford Exhibition, and the same bird paintings were on show)

Appendix VIII

1974   **Lancaster City Museum**

**The Local Scene – circa 1900 : paintings by
Reginald Aspinwall, Robert Rampling and William Woodhouse.**
6th – 27th April 1974

A combined total of eighty-three works were on view.
No Catalogue was produced for this exhibition.

1975   **The McDonald Booth Gallery Ltd.**
Exhibition - William Woodhouse (1857-1939)
Pencil, Watercolour and Oil Sketches and Paintings from the Artist's family
Collection.
13th November – 29th November 1975

Oil Paintings:

1	"At the End of the Day".
2	English Setter and Game.
3	Grey Working Pony.
4	Cumbrian Landscape.
5	A Fox Terrier.
6	Studies of Foxes.
	(Vo.) Sailing Vessel Coming Into Port.
7	Head of a Pointer.
8	Mares and Foal.
	(Vo.) Bison at Sunset.
9	Studies of Cattle.
	(Vo.) Cow Resting.
10	Studies of a Foal.
11	Highland Bull.
12	Still-life – Corncrake.
13	An Ayrshire Cow.
14	View across the Bay to the Cumbrian Hills.
15	Studies of Rooks and Foxes.
16	Highland Bull on the Move.
17	Irish Water Spaniel and Snipe.
18	African Lion at Night near the Camp Fire.
19	Bison. *(Vo.)*
20	Blackbird's Nest in the Hedgerow.
21	Moorhen at the Edge of the Flight Pool.
22	Roe Heads – a pair.
23	Still-life – Roe Buck.
24	Still-life – Fallow Deer.
25	Head of an Airedale.
26	Still-life – Mallard and Teal.
27	Study of a Foal.
28	Porpoises off Coll and Tiree.
29	A Foal.
30	Study of a Horse.
31	Stalking Sketch – an impression.
32	Field Spaniel retrieving a Mallard.
32a.	"The Perils of War".

Watercolour Drawings:

33   Cocker Spaniel.

34   Oystercatcher.

35   The Old Forest-Tree.

36   Sheep Studies.

37   A Badger.

38   A Cow Resting in the Meadow.

39   Study sheet of Vultures, Crowned Crane, and Purple Gallinule.

40   An Ayrshire Cow.

41   Two Shelduck Young and a Scaup Duck.

42   Two Studies of Pigeon Breeds and a Lop-Eared Rabbit.

43   Young Corncrake.

44   An Ayrshire Cow.

45   Peacock & *(Vo.)* Toucan.

46   Horned Sheep on the Hills.

47   Otter Hounds.

48   Zoological Studies.

49   Sheep and Lamb Studies.

50   Otter Hounds.

51   Two Calf Studies.

52   A Dromedary.

53   A Terrier Asleep.

54   A Lion Asleep.

55   Man-Eating Tiger on the Defensive.

56   Head of a Stag.

57   Head of a Springer Spaniel.

58   Studies of Goats at Rest.

59   Study of a Lion's Head.

60   "In the Byre".

61   Studies of Goats.

62   Study of a Working Horse.

63   Man-Eating Tiger Approaching the Trap.

64   Studies of Highland Cattle.

65   Cock and Hen Pheasant in Winter.

66   The Return from the Tiger Hunt.

67   Tiger and Rhinoceros.

68   "The Deerstalker's Pony".

Pencil Sketches:

69   Tiger Studies. *(Double sided)*
70   Sea Lion Studies.
71   Lion and Lioness.
72   Dogs Playing.
73   Lion Studies. *(Double sided)*
74   Wolf.
75   Lioness and Cubs.
76   Guernsey Cow Study.
77   Recumbent Tiger.
78   Pony and Dogs.
79   Studies of Cattle. *(Double sided)*
80   Bison Kneeling.
81   Multiple Studies of Animals and Birds.
82   Musk Ox.
83   Chamois.
84   Racoon.
85   Bear.
86   Studies of Donkeys.
              (Vo.) Working Pony in Harness.
87   Racoon Studies.
88   Studies of Monkeys.
89   Studies of Sheep.
90   Studies of Goats.
91   Circus Elephants being washed.
92   Studies of Calves.
93   Terrier Studies.
94   Bull and Cows.
95   Studies of Highland Cattle.
96   Studies of Otters.
97   Calves Lying by a Farm Wagon.
98   Studies of Goats.
99   Coursing Study.
100   Oystercatchers.
101   Farm Collies.
102   A Foxhound.
103   Multiple Studies of a Terrier, Foxes and a Horse being Twitched.
104   Studies of Wild Cattle.
105   Highland Cattle in the Snow.
106   Studies of Gannets.
107   Two Studies of Goats.
108   Studies of Jack Snipe and a Partridge Head.
109   Studies of Sheep.
110   Studies of Elephants and Dromedaries.

111	Studies of a Terrier.
112	Studies of a Bull.
113	Studies of a Collie and Sheep.
114	Studies of Donkeys.
115	Studies of Sheep.

(Some of the above sketches are now in the Woodhouse Collection at the Lancaster City Museum and form part of their large collection of William's pencil drawings).

Appendix X

1977   **Cumbrian Fine Arts, Kirkby Lonsdale, Cumbria**
An Exhibition of Paintings and Drawings.
26th November to 17th December 1977.

Oil Paintings:

1	An Eagle Owl attacking a Mouse.
2	"Vanquished".
3	Portrait of Maria Elizabeth Woodhouse - oval.
4	Self Portrait of The Artist as a young man.
5	Portrait of Roy Woodhouse on the battlefield in 1916.
6	Portrait of a fisherman.
7	An Irish Water Spaniel with a Mallard.
8	A Lion in the undergrowth.
9	Spaniel with a Grouse.
10	Head of a Terrier inscribed "Gyp".
11	Crow Duffy Farm.
12	Tinkers on Heysham Head.
13	Study of a Roe Deer.
14	Study of a Bull. *(Vo.)* A portrait and an animal study.
15	Study of cows. *(Vo.)* Studies of lions and birds inscribed "London Zoo".
16	The Government Bull.
17	Head of a Wolfhound.
18	A Jay.
19	Study of a donkey.
20	The Old Stone Pier at Morecambe.
21	A Tinker with a Parakeet in a cage.
22	Team of eight horses pulling a timber wagon.
23	"Perils of War".
24	Farmyard with mare and foal.
24a	The Huntsmans Return. *(His pony and two dogs outside a cottage)*

Watercolours:

25	A Roebuck startled by an eagle.
26	Tram Horses at Morecambe.
27	H.M.S. Akbar.
28	Study of Camels.
29	The old village and church at Heysham.
30	Fallen trees.
31	The shore at Heysham.
32	Sketch of old Heysham.
33	Ballerina on a circus pony. *(Painted on the back of a time sheet)*
34	View of Port Said.

35	Sketch of Borwick Hall.
36	A Jay.
37	Sparrows.
38	A Caique on the Bosphorus.
39	Sketch of a St. Bernard.
40	The fruit market at Port Said, dated 1889.
41	Sketch of a sailing ship.
42	Sketch for H.M.S. Akbar.
43	Hateley Shoot, Bamborough Cliffs. *(This was probably a preliminary drawing for the frontispiece of 'Birds of Yorkshire')*
44	Hares. N.F.S.
45	A Haystack with sheep resting and farmers ploughing in the background. N.F.S.
46	The Wheelhouse.
47	Port Said, dated 1889.
48	Port Said. *(Vo.)* Studies of Egyptian mules.
49	Camel Studies, inscribed.
50	Camel and elephant studies, inscribed. *(Vo.)* Study of a Camel.
51	Sketch of sheep in Egyptian town.
51a	Cottages at Heysham with Children seated by a Horse and Cart.
51b	A Spaniel lying on a Settee.

Drawings:

52	Sketches of Horses, probably at Port Said.
53	Mare and foal.
54	Chillingham Cattle.
55	"Old Caravan to Skipton".
56	A tram horse.
57	Study of a horse's head. *(Together with a copy made by Roy Woodhouse in preparation for an etching, and the etching)*
58	Arab horses and rider.
59	Sketch inscribed "Jim Baxter, shrimping home".
60	An Inn, inscribed and monogrammed.
61	Turkish boats at Port Said.
62	Sketches of "The Moss Brow".
63	Egyptian cattle market. (Vo) Studies of Egyptian domestic animals.
64	Central Pier and Old Winter Gardens inscribed "Trawler in Storm".
65	Study of sheep. *(The artist has used the bottom of this drawing as a palette)*
66	The market place at Skipton.
67	Bruges.
68	Canal scene, possibly Skipton.
69	Tollesby Cleveland, inscribed and dated May 27/90.
70	Ilston Grange, Leicestershire.
71	Study of a cow in a byre.

72	Three Egyptian Cattle market studies.
73	The Smithy.
74	Studies of Rabbits.
75	Wash drawing of a lady sewing.
76	York.
77	A Man and his dog inscribed "Silverdale".
78	The Knackers Yard.
79	Dog cart at Bruges before the journey.
80	Dog cart at Bruges, after the journey.
81	A Setter, signed. *(This is an early drawing possibly executed whilst the artist was still at school)*
82	Three eastern studies.
83	Oxen tethered to wheel.
84	Sand camels in the Suez Canal, inscribed. *(Vo.)* Sand carriers.
85	Sketch of horses.
86	Dock scene at Port Said, inscribed.
87	Egyptian water carrier.

Also on view were:

A Linthorpe Vase, hand painted by William Woodhouse portraying an avocet. This vase is now in the Linthorpe collection held at the Dorman Museum, Middlesbrough.

A terracotta sculpture of a Bison (the only piece of sculpture to be signed by Woodhouse).

Front cover for "The Field" (magazine).

The telegram sent to Woodhouse in Bremerhaven advising him that his painting "Doomed" had been accepted by the Royal Academy.

The artist's log of his voyage to the Middle East in 1889 aboard "Moss Brow" and his return journey on the "Lizzie English".

2 Volumes, "Birds of Yorkshire", by Thomas Nelson and W. Eagle-Clarke, Frontispieces and Sketches by William Woodhouse.

Appendix XI

1981   **Lancaster City Museum Exhibition**
                 A Century's Span – William and R.B.E. Woodhouse.
                 2nd August to 26th September 1981.

Catalogue of William's paintings: (Numbers as they appear in the catalogue)

1   Cattle. *(An early work by William Woodhouse)*
2   Robert Baxter, his horse and dog. *(Painted in 1877 the earliest known dated work by William Woodhouse)*
3   Stable Companions.
4   Majestic. *(A horse owned by the Blacker Family dated December 1909)*
5   Army Horses in Stables near Heysham Tower, during The First World War.
6   Horses being shod in the Smithy on the Stone Jetty at Morecambe circa 1890.
7   Moorland Ponies and Grouse.
8   Groom and Horses.
9   Tramway Horses.
10   Lakeland Bridge.
11   Beamsley Beacon and the River Wharfe.
12   Teal, Drake and Two Ducks.
13   Wood Pigeons.
14   A Lane in Heysham.
15   A Farm at Heysham.
16   Cart Horses going to a Horse Fair.
17   In Borwick Hall – a Romance.
18   Staithes, Yorkshire.
19   Heysham in Snow.
20   Heysham, a sketch.
21   Heysham, Cliffs and St. Patrick's Chapel.
22   Canal Bridge, Hest Bank (1).
23   Canal Bridge, Hest Bank (2).
29   Lupins.
30   Stocks.
31   Geraniums and Pansies.
32   1889, first acceptance by the Royal Academy – Doomed.
39   Grouse Shot in Flight.
43   'Auburn', *(the Artist's Home from 1902 until his Death in 1939)* and St. John's Church, Heysham.
44   Roy (R.B.E.) Woodhouse, at the Front in 1916.
46   Silverdale Church, from the Sitting Room of Hawthorn Banks.
47   Silverdale, Roy's Home, Hawthorn Banks.
48   The Hall at Auburn. *(As William knew it)*

49	Garden Seat, Auburn.
50	Kenilcote. *(The Artist's Home until 1902)*
51	Marie Winifred, the daughter of William Woodhouse, painted by her Father circa 1900, aged about 5.
53	The Artist's Wife, Maria Elizabeth Woodhouse.
54	The Donkey Boy.
55	Grouse.
56	A Retriever. *(William Woodhouse painted in 1912. Whilst his owner's small son was being taken for a walk by the canal, he fell in. Rufus, the retriever pulled him out)*
57	Spaniel with Game.
58	Vanquished. *(Exhibited in the Royal Academy 1911)*
59	Bison and Wolves.

Appendix XII

1989-1990   **Lancaster City Museum**
'A Great Love of Nature' – the artistry of William Woodhouse
1857-1939.
9th October 1989 – 10th February 1990.

Oil Paintings:
'Lunch-Time'. *(A pair of setters with guns and game bag)*
Robert Baxter with his Horse and Dog, 1877. *(The artist's earliest dated work)*
Shrimping in the Snow.
The Church at Brookhouse.
Three Horses at a Water Trough.
Jess and Game 1886.
Cormorant and its Chicks, Mona's Isle.
Partridges in the Snow.
Self Portrait.
Threshing Machine.
Orvar. *(The Artist's elkhound)*
Army horses in a Stable with Groom.
Spaniel (Kim) with Game Birds and Rabbit.
Study of Horse. *(Oil sketch)*.
Tiger.
Hannah Woodhouse. *(Oil sketch of the Artist's Mother)*
Constantinople from the Sea.
Portrait of the Artist's Wife in Peasant Costume. *(Maria Elizabeth with Peacocks)*
Marie Winifred as a Young Woman.
Landscape after Bercham.
Army Horses at Heysham Cliffs during the 1914-1918 War.
Oxen in Yoke. *(Oil sketch)*
'Vanquished'. *(Last RA painting)*
The Donkey Boy. *(Lancaster City Museums – Gift of the Artist)*
Portrait of Maria Elizabeth with shawl. *(Lancaster City Museums)*

Watercolour Paintings:
Sunderland Point with the Cotton Tree.
Hayrick, Sheep and Gentleman Sowing Seed.
Fishing Baulks at Heysham.
The 'Vangelis' with Haulers. *(At Half Moon Bay)*
Grouse in Flight.
Cattle in Pasture.
Maria Elizabeth, the artist's fiancée 1889. *(Draped in a cloak possibly brought back from his travels in the Near East)*
Musselling on Morecambe Bay.

Harvesting - Haymaking at Caton.

Eagle and Hare.

Springing Leopard and Hunter. *(Watercolour sketch, possibly intended as an illustration for W.S. Chadwick's 'Life Stories of Big Game' 1930)*

Morecambe Front with Winter Gardens and Old Central Pier.

HMS Akbar at Ward's Shipbreaking Yard, Morecambe.

Santa Sophia Mosque Steps, Constantinople.

Morecambe Tram Horse.

Heysham.

Horse with Stag.

Building the Bonfire on Heysham Cliffs. *(Part of local celebrations for the Coronation of George V, 1911)*

Winnie Woodhouse.

Heysham in the Snow. *(Haworth Art Gallery, Accrington)*

The Blacksmith 1939. *(Woodhouse's last Painting)*

Overton Church.

Off Algiers 6 April 1889.

Duart Castle at Mull.

Oxen in Egypt.

The Shrimpers. *(Shrimpers on Morecambe Bay – Harris Museum & Art Gallery Preston)*

'Kenilcote'. *(The artist's home in Chatsworth Road, with cornfield)*

The Hall at Auburn.

Horse Drovers.

Pencil Sketch:

Self Portrait with Animals.

Pen and Ink:

Quayside Scene Port Said, 1889.

Other Items:

Antlers. *(Hornby Women's Institute)*

Game Bag.

Cartridge Bag.

Black Buck Mounted Head. *(Previously owned by W Woodhouse)*

Roe Deer in Winter Coat.

The Birds of Yorkshire by Thomas H Nelson. *(Two volumes 1907 with frontispiece and several illustrations by Woodhouse)*

Woodhouse's Travel Diary.

Woodhouse's Tripod Stool.

Terracotta Head of Maria Elizabeth Woodhouse.

Panel on 'Doomed'. *(Woodhouse's first RA Painting)*

Selection of Exhibition Catalogues - Fine Art Society etc.

Selection of Correspondence regarding commissions.

Carved Oak Settle.
Leopard Skin.
Linthorpe Vase with Avocet.
Log of the Stella.
Terracotta Stag's Head.
Photograph of 'The Taxidermist'. *(A portrait of George Mussell)*
Photograph – after a day's hunting. *(The artist with an unidentified companion early 20th century)*
Photograph – the artist's Photograph – the artist's wife with her mother, Sarah Emsley and her children Winnie and Roy. *(Early 20th century)*

Zouave Jacket brought back from the Near East by Woodhouse, 1889.
Photograph of Woodhouse Family. *(Three generations with Hannah Woodhouse)*
Photograph of the drawing room at 'Kenilcote'.
'Dressings' for studio, including two stuffed bird arrangements, two guns, easel, chair, table, sculpture of Hercules, 4 pieces oriental ceramics, lidded pewter cup. *(Lancaster City Museums, School Service and King's Own Royal Regiment Museum).*

Appendix XIII

1990   **Studio Arts Gallery**
Exhibition of Oils, Watercolours and Drawings
by William Woodhouse 1857 – 1939.
26th March – 31st March 1990.

Oil Paintings:

		£
1.	Vale of Lune Hunt, Gone Away.	8,750
2.	Black Terrier Dog with Rabbit.	14,000
3.	"Kim" Chipperke - A Dutch Barge Dog.	9,800
4.	Jess and Turk, Waiting for Master.	16,500
5.	Cocker Spaniel with Game.	24,000
6.	The Unexpected Encounter.	16,500
7.	Study of a Pony.	500
8.	Deer Hound with Stag.	6,800
9.	Cattle Cooling Off.	1,650

Watercolours:

10.	Red Grouse.	6,750
11.	Morecambe Bay, from Heysham Rocks.	1,200
12.	Bempton Cliffs looking over to Filey Brigg. *(Dated 1909)*	1,200
13.	*(No painting listed)*	
14.	Approach to Shore, Heysham.	2,250
15.	Tiger and Rhino.	1,650
16.	Pair of Waders.	950
17.	Washing Day, Heysham.	1,850
18.	The Stride.	450
19.	The Wild Fowler.	475
20.	Evening on Morecambe Bay.	825
21.	Deer in Levens Park.	Not for sale
22.	The Sly Fox.	5,850
23A.	Heysham under Snow. }	
23B.	Heysham early Spring. } *(Pair)*	4,300
24.	Badger.	3,950

Sketches:
Watercolour, Pencil, Pen and Ink:

			£
25.	Embsay Moor, Yorkshire.	*(Watercolour)*	225
26.	Cavalry under Attack.	*(Watercolour)*	265
27.	Borwick Hall.	*(Watercolour)*	125
28.	South of Redcar.	*(Pencil)*	125
29.	The Old Stone Jetty, Morecambe.	*(Pencil)*	125
30.	Lady Sewing.	*(Watercolour)*	180
31.	Akbar Old Harbour.	*(Pencil/Watercolour)*	680
32.	Parrots.	*(Watercolour)*	225
33.	Tram Horses at Morecambe.	*(Pencil)*	425
34.	Head of Boy.	*(Pencil)*	75
35.	Buffalo with Tiger.	*(Pencil)*	125
36.	Studies on Bison.	*(Pencil)*	75
37.	Studies on Lady.	*(Pencil)*	125
38.	Old Caravan to Skipton.	*(Pencil)*	75
39.	Tram Horse Feeding from Nosebag.	*(Pencil)*	75
40.	A Street in York.	*(Pencil)*	125
41.	Lune Side.	*(Pen and Ink)*	245
42.	A Fisherman.	*(Pencil)*	75
43.	Moss Brow, leaving Cardiff March 29th 1889.	*(Pencil)*	75
44.	Bruges, Belguim.	*(Pencil)*	115
45.	Port Said 1889.	*(Ink and Crayon)*	310
46.	Tiger Approaching Trap.	*(Watercolour)*	545
47.	Colonel Baillies Stables, Ilston Grange, Leicestershire.	*(Pencil and Ink)*	110
48.	Old Hall, Cleveland May 27th 1890.	*(Pencil)*	110
49.	Study of Tram Horses.	*(Pencil and Ink)*	85
50.	A Man and his Dog, Silverdale.	*(Pencil and Ink)*	75
51.	A Vet at Work.	*(Pencil)*	85
52.	St. Bernard in the Mountains.	*(Pencil and Watercolour)*	180
53.	Study of Pigs. (a)	*(Pencil)*	95
54.	Study of Pigs. (b)	*(Pencil)*	95
55.	Study of Pigs. (c)	*(Pencil)*	95
56.	Study of Pig.	*(Pencil)*	75
57.	Study of Cattle. (a)	*(Pencil and Ink)*	85
58.	Study of Cattle. (b)	*(Pencil and Ink)*	85
59.	Central Pier, Morecambe.	*(Pencil)*	105

Appendix XIV

1998	**Fine Art in Focus** **Lancaster City Museum** 25th April to 6th June 1998.	
		Lancaster Museum Accession and negative numbers
	A Selection of Working Drawings.	LM 90.43
	A Portrait of Maria Elizabeth Woodhouse, the Artist's wife.	LM 96.50/19
	A Portrait of Marie Winifred Woodhouse, the Artist's daughter.	LM 96.50/10
	Driving Horses to Market.	LM 90.50/20
	Hallway of 'Auburn' Heysham, the Artist's home.	LM 90.50/8
	Woman's Head, after Lawrence.	LM 96.50/2
	Army Horses at Heysham, 1914-18 War.	LM 90.50/11
	Heysham Village in the Snow.	LM 90.50/14
	'Auburn' with St. John's Church.	LM 90.50/15
	Oystercatchers.	LM 87.54/1
	Skipton from the Canal.	LM 91.11/1
	Painted Bedhead.	LM 96/50/35

Miscellaneous Exhibitions

A couple of pieces of exhibition material were unfortunately undated.

1.   **Exhibition of Paintings – Blackpool**

An exhibition of paintings by Lancashire artists promoted by Blackpool Sketching Club and Arts and Crafts Society under the auspices of the Blackpool Corporation.
Woodhouse had four paintings hung at the exhibition.

2.   **(1890's)?   The 6th Exhibition of the North British Academy of Arts, held at the Crystal Palace, Sydenham**

His Grace the Duke of Rutland opened the exhibition, which was called 'Dog in Art',
Woodhouse's painting 'Setter with Game' was highly commended and appeared at several later exhibitions.

Please note that all prices quoted for paintings in this book should not be used to assess their current value.

Illustrations and Photographs

List of Exhibitions 1881 – to date

Lancaster Exhibition circa 1881.
Royal Scottish Academy Exhibition 1883.
Institute of Painters in Oils 1889.
Royal Academy of Arts 1889.
North British Academy of Arts Exhibition, Sydenham (Crystal Palace) 1890's.
The Second Annual Art Exhibition of Pictures in Oils and Watercolours Lancaster 1894.
The Third Annual Art Exhibition of Pictures in Oils and Watercolours Lancaster 1895.
Walker Art Gallery, Liverpool.
Royal Academy of Arts 1896
Derby Corporation Art Gallery 1896.
Royal Birmingham Society of Artist's Exhibition 1896.
Lancaster Exhibition 1908.
Royal Academy of Arts 1911.
Royal Institute of Painters in Watercolours 1911.
Royal Institute of Painters in Watercolours 1925.
41st Spring Exhibition of Modern Art at the Atkinson Gallery, Southport 1926.
Annual Spring Exhibition of Lancashire Artists, Preston 1927, 1928, 1929, 1930.
Lancaster Exhibition (all paintings by W. & R.B.E. Woodhouse) 1931.
Annual Spring Exhibition of Lancashire Artists, Preston 1931, 1932, 1933.
Heysham Exhibition 1933.
Oxford Exhibition 1934.
Bristol Exhibition 1934.
Annual Spring Exhibition of Lancashire Artists, Preston 1934, 1935, 1936, 1937.
Annual Spring Exhibition of Lancashire Art, Preston 1939, 1940, 1943, 1944, 1949.
Lancaster City Museum Exhibition 1974.
McDonald Booth Gallery Exhibition 1975.
Cumbrian Fine Arts Exhibition, Kirkby Lonsdale 1977.
The Lower Nupend Gallery, near Malvern 1980.
Lancaster City Museum Exhibition 1981.
Lancaster City Museum Exhibition 1989
Studio Arts Gallery Lancaster 1990
Lancaster City Museum Exhibition 1998.

Bibliography

Aspects of Lancaster	edited by Sue Wilson.	2002
Birds of Yorkshire	by Thomas H. Nelson.	1907
The Dog in Art	by Nick Waters.	
Four Centuries of British Art	by Sidney Parviere.	
From Lancaster to the Lakes - An Essay	by David Steel.	1992
The Growth of Morecambe: Morecambe Visitor Publication.	by T. E. Potter.	1976
The History of Heysham	by F. Whewell Hogarth.	1934
The History of Morecambe and Heysham.	by R.C. Quick.	
Lancaster Morecambe & Heysham	by Nigel Dalziel & Susan Ashworth.	2001
Life Stories of Big Game	by W.S. Chadwick.	1928
Lost Resort, The Flow and Ebb of Morecambe	by Roger. K. Bingham.	1990
Mishi the Maneater	by E.C. Stuart-Baker	Circa. 1930
Morecambe, Alias Poulton-le-Sands, A Dip into the Past, A Study	by Beverley Grimes.	
The Morecambe Bay Wildfowlers Association. The First 75 Years	by Terry Thorpe and Brian Hill	1995
Shipbreaking at Morecambe, T.W. Ward Ltd. 1905-1933	by Ian Buxton and Nigel Dalziel.	1993
Storeys of Lancaster	by Guy Christie.	1964
Yorkshire Pots and Potteries	by Heather Lawrence	1974

General Register Indexes for Births, Marriages and Deaths

Newspapers and Journals
Lancaster Guardian	July 1895
Morecambe Visitor, Heysham Chronicle and Lancaster Advertiser	21st October 1925
Preston Guardian	12th April 1930
Lancaster Guardian	12th June 1931
Lancaster Observer and Morecambe Chronicle	12th June 1931
Morecambe & Heysham Visitor, and Lancaster Advertiser	10th June 1931
Yorkshire Post	9th June 1931
Morecambe & Heysham Visitor, and Lancaster Advertiser	27th September 1933
Morecambe & Heysham Visitor, and Lancaster Advertiser	4th October 1933
Morecambe Visitor	18th January 1939
The Field	17th November 1966
The Field	13th July 1975
Shooting Times and Country Magazine	13th November 1975
Morecambe Guardian	18th November 1975
Morecambe Visitor	2nd September 1981
Morecambe Guardian	4th September 1981
The Visitor	4th March 1987
Lancashire Evening Post	18th December 1987
The Visitor	10th January 1990
The Lakes Journal	August 1990
The Visitor	9th February 1994
Dog World	July 2002

Lancashire Life:
Portrait of a Perfectionist	by Roy Gudgeon	January 1986
William Woodhouse	by Roy Gudgeon	

Black and White, a weekly illustrated review incorporating The Pictorial World	27th May 1893

Exhibition Catalogues:
Catalogues of the Annual Spring Exhibitions of Paintings by Lancashire Artists 1927 to 1937, 1939 and 1949.

Catalogue of a Loan Exhibition by William Woodhouse
5th December - 31st December 1927

Heysham Ex-Council Rooms -Exhibition of Oil Paintings and Watercolours by William Woodhouse 1933

Borough of Lancaster – Exhibition of Oils, Watercolours and Dry Points by William Woodhouse and R.B.E. Woodhouse
9th July - 22nd July 1931

McDonald Booth Gallery Ltd. Exhibition -.William Woodhouse
13th November - 29th November 1975

Cumbrian Fine Arts Gallery, An Exhibition of Paintings and Drawings William Woodhouse
26th November - 17th December 1977

The Nupend Gallery, Christmas Exhibition
6th December - 14th December 1980

Lancaster City Museums Exhibition. A Century's Span, William and R.B.E. Woodhouse
2nd August - 26th September 1981

Lancaster City Museums Exhibition. A Great Love of Nature, the Artistry of William Woodhouse
9th October1989 - 10th February 1990

Studio Arts Gallery, Lancaster. Exhibition of Oils, Watercolours and Drawings by William Woodhouse 26th March – 31st March 1990

Harris Reference Library – Lancashire County Libraries and Information Service Central Division.
Lancaster Reference Library – Lancashire County Libraries and Information Service Northern Division.
Morecambe Reference Library – Lancashire County Libraries and Information Service Northern Division.

Census Returns   1841 – 1901.

The Author – Pam Corder-Birch

Pam, born at the Royal Infirmary, Lancaster, has lived and worked in the South East of England all her life. Her love for Morecambe and surrounding area is 'in the blood'- family ties resulting in holidays to the resort every year since she was a small child. As a Member of the Lancashire Family History and Heraldry Society, Essex, Sussex and Bradford Family History Societies, Pam enjoys all aspects of genealogy. A keen interest in Woodhouse paintings and the family connection has led to her writing this book. After living and working for many years in London, Pam returned to the Essex/Suffolk border where she met and married Adrian. Following many years in the legal profession he is now employed in local government and is a respected local historian and author of several books. Pam shares Adrian's love for local history, being a member of the Halstead and District Local History Society. As a keen gardener, much of her spare time is spent working in their woodland garden.

INDEX

204

Postscript:

Well into the Millennium I was walking round a very historic location close to where I live, showing friends the Guildhall, and other national delights within the village of Lavenham, Suffolk. Ambling through the streets, gazing in the windows as we sauntered along, we came across The Wildlife Art Gallery, which was holding an exhibition. It looked very interesting so we ventured in. Imagine our surprise when we saw five paintings by William Woodhouse for sale. The exhibition's aim was to represent the work of leading wildlife artists spanning the last one hundred and fifty years.

2002   The Wildlife Art Gallery, Lavenham, Suffolk
Wildlife and the Artist.
October 27th – November 25th 2002

1   Moorhen
2   Snipe & teal
3   Water rail
4   Stoats
5   The raider (depicts a fox stealing away with a cockerel in its mouth)

Therefore the work of William Woodhouse continues to create interest throughout the country in this new millennium. I should be pleased to hear from any reader who has any additional information about William Woodhouse, his family and work.

Moorhen. Watercolour.
Private collection